LUCENT LIBRARY OF
**BLACK HISTORY**

# THE STORY OF
# AFRICAN AMERICAN
# MUSIC

By Andrew Pina

Portions of this book originally appeared in
*From Ragtime to Hip-Hop: A Century of Black American Music* by Adam Woog.

LUCENT
PRESS

Published in 2018 by
**Lucent Press, an Imprint of Greenhaven Publishing, LLC**
353 3rd Avenue
Suite 255
New York, NY 10010

Designer: Deanna Paternostro
Editor: Siyavush Saidian

**Library of Congress Cataloging-in-Publication Data**

Names: Pina, Andrew.
Title: The story of African American music / Andrew Pina.
Description: New York : Lucent Press, [2018] | Series: Lucent library of
  black history | Includes bibliographical references and index.
Identifiers: LCCN 2017011793 | ISBN 9781534560734 (library bound book)
Subjects: LCSH: African Americans–Music–History and criticism. | Popular
  music–United States–History and criticism.
Classification: LCC ML3479 .P56 2018 | DDC 780.89/96073–dc23
LC record available at https://lccn.loc.gov/2017011793

Printed in the United States of America

CPSIA compliance information: Batch #BS17KL: For further information contact Greenhaven Publishing LLC, New York, New York at 1-844-317-7404.

Please visit our website, www.greenhavenpublishing.com. For a free color catalog of all our
high-quality books, call toll free 1-844-317-7404 or fax 1-844-317-7405.

# CONTENTS

# FOREWORD

**B**lack men and women in the United States have become successful in every field, but they have faced incredible challenges while striving for that success. They have overcome racial barriers, violent prejudice, and hostility on every side, all while continuing to advance technology, literature, the arts, and much more.

From medicine and law to sports and literature, African Americans have come to excel in every industry. However, the story of African Americans has often been one of prejudice and persecution. More than 300 years ago, Africans were taken in chains from their home and enslaved to work for the earliest American settlers. They suffered for more than two centuries under the brutal oppression of their owners, until the outbreak of the American Civil War in 1861. After the dust settled four years later and thousands of Americans—both black and white—had died in combat, slavery in the United States had been legally abolished. By the turn of the 20th century, with the help of the 13th, 14th, and 15th Amendments to the U.S. Constitution, African American men had finally won significant battles for the basic rights of citizenship. Then, with the passage of the groundbreaking Civil Rights Act of 1964, many people of all races began to believe that America was finally ready to start moving toward a more equal future.

These triumphs of human equality were achieved with help from brave social activists such as Frederick Douglass, Martin Luther King Jr., and Maya Angelou. They all experienced racial prejudice in their lifetimes and fought by writing, speaking, and peacefully acting against it. By exposing the suffering of the black community, they brought the United States together to try to remedy centuries' worth of wrongdoing. Today, it is important to learn about the history of African Americans and their experiences in modern America in order to work toward healing the divide that still exists in the United States. This series aims to give readers a deeper appreciation for and understanding of a part of the American story that is often left untold.

Even before the legal emancipation of slaves, black culture was thriving despite many attempts to suppress it. From the 1600s to 1800s, slaves developed their own cultural perspective. From music, to language, to art, slaves began cultivating an identity that was completely unique. Soon after these slaves were granted citizenship and were integrated into American society, African American culture burst into the mainstream. New generations of authors, scholars, painters, and singers were born, and they spread an appreciation for black culture across America and the entire world. Studying the contributions of these talented individuals fosters a sense of optimism. Despite the cruel treatment and racist attitudes they faced, these men and women never gave up, changing the world with their determination and unique voice. Discovering the triumphs and tragedies of the oppressed allows readers to gain a clearer picture of American history and American cultural identity.

Here to help young readers with this discovery, this series offers a glimpse into the lives and accomplishments of some of the most important and influential African Americans across historical time periods. Titles examine primary source documents and quotes from contemporary thinkers and observers to provide a full and nuanced learning experience for readers. With thoroughly researched text, unique sidebars, and a carefully selected bibliography for further research, this series is an invaluable resource for young scholars. Moreover, it does not shy away from reconciling the brutality of the past with a sense of hopefulness for the future. This series provides critical tools for understanding more about how black history is a vital part of American history.

# SETTING THE SCENE:

**1600–1800**
Spirituals develop as a form of African American folk music.

**1871**
The Fisk Jubilee Singers are formed; African American music spreads nationwide.

| 1600–1800 | 1843 | 1871 | 1890–1920 | 1935–1945 |
|---|---|---|---|---|

**1890–1920**
Blues, ragtime, and jazz develop; gospel music develops from spirituals.

**1843**
The first racist minstrel shows begin touring the United States.

**1935–1945**
Swing develops as a dominant subgenre of jazz.

# A TIMELINE

**1950–1969**
Soul develops out of R&B; the British Invasion inspires renewed American interest in blues.

**1990–2000**
Hip-hop continues to evolve and Jay Z becomes a popular figure; new forms of R&B also continue to develop.

1950–1969          1980–1989          1990–2000          2003–2017

**1980–1989**
Hip-hop and rap develop; Michael Jackson, Prince, and Whitney Houston emerge as prominent solo pop artists.

**2003–2017**
Hip-hop diversifies; Kanye West, Beyoncé, Drake, and others emerge as dominant forces in popular music.

# INTRODUCTION

# A CENTURY AND A HALF OF MUSIC

The diversity of genres of black popular music throughout the past century and a half has been wide-ranging: spirituals, ragtime, gospel, swing, bebop, country blues, electric blues, rhythm and blues, soul, funk, new jack swing, neo-soul, rap, hip-hop, and more. These genres have influenced each other through the decades and have influenced music made by other cultures in the United States and beyond.

As it has evolved, black American music has come to dominate popular music. Repeatedly overlooked as the pastime of an oppressed minority, now it is the single most significant influence on all American pop music—and, by extension, on world music as well. Without black musicians, there would be no rock and roll, no blues, no jazz, no soul or funk, nor would hip-hop be one of the dominant genres of current popular music.

Indeed, many observers feel that black popular music is among America's greatest cultural achievements and an important influence throughout the world. Jazz trumpeter Wynton Marsalis once commented, "The uniquely American legacy of swing and blues [is] a history to be valued, an artistic achievement that is on par with the most magnificent works of Western classical music."[1]

## Feeling the Music

Marsalis mentions only two of black popular music's subgenres. These various types of music have obvious differences but also frequently blend, with overlaps that make them difficult to differentiate or categorize. On the other hand, much of the fun of listening to music is spotting both differences and common ground—discovering, for example, what separates or binds together blues and swing music.

*Wynton Marsalis is remarkable not just for his inspiring trumpet playing but also because he is an outspoken supporter of classical jazz traditions.*

all pack an emotional punch. The emotion might be sadness or happiness, anger or exhilaration, yearning or satisfaction. No matter what it is, it is always there. Aretha Franklin, known as the Queen of Soul, and other prominent African American artists have all said that the feelings and emotions of life are always a centerpiece of their music.

Even casual listening reveals that, despite their differences, the many genres of African American popular music have some basic elements in common. The most vital of these bring listeners back to the musical traditions of Africa. Such characteristics as complex rhythms and the use of "blue notes" are directly descended from music brought to North America by slaves. Named for the blues genre, blue notes are a "variable ... lowering of the third, seventh, and occasionally fifth [notes] of the major scale."[2] In essence, these notes are unexpected to the ear.

Subgenres of black music share another important characteristic: They

## First Ignored, Then Embraced

African American music, like other types of music, has evolved over time. One style emerged from the one that came before it, keeping some aspects of it, changing some, and creating an entirely new sound. These changes can happen slowly, over years of development. However, such changes can also be startlingly fast.

A major change in African American pop music occurred as the 19th century ended and the 20th century began.

# CONFLICTS IN SONG

To deeply religious people, the differences between gospel, jazz, and blues were obvious and offensive. They felt that the rhythms and melodies of jazz and blues songs were sinfully suggestive. They were also disgusted by the message this music sent. To some, jazz represented open wickedness and blues was the sound of despair. In contrast, spiritual music delivered a message of stability, hope, happiness, and love, all delivered through God. As the legendary gospel singer Mahalia Jackson once commented, "Somebody singing blues is crying out of a pit. I'm singing out of the joy of my salvation."[1]

1. Quoted in Anthony Heilbut, *The Gospel Sound: Good News and Bad Times.* New York, NY: Limelight, 1997, p. 299.

*One of the best known gospel singers of all time, Mahalia Jackson's musical talent came from her passion and deep emotion.*

Before then, the music was commonly folk style, encompassing both religious and nonreligious songs and generally familiar only to black audiences. Mainstream audiences—white American audiences—knew that style of music only through a form of entertainment called minstrel shows. These were racist shows, commonly put on by white actors wearing dark black makeup. Minstrel shows reinforced stereotypes against African Americans.

Within a few decades, however, three major genres—jazz, blues, and gospel—developed in black communities and attracted a wide audience. This began the process of black music breaking into the American musical mainstream. Over the next decades, jazz, blues, and gospel evolved within their own boundaries.

The fast-paced jazz of the early 20th

century, for instance, morphed into a style called swing. This new, popular subgenre seemed to pop into existence overnight. The jazz clubs in American cities transformed into swing clubs. After a few years, swing, in turn, quickly went out of fashion to make way for the next major jazz style. This was repeated many times and across many genres. The 1900s were a time of rapid, significant change in black music.

In its earliest years, however, African American music did not change quickly. In fact, it seemed to barely change at all. During the slave era, black popular music was simply whatever slaves sang, and white slaveholders largely ignored it. Because of the racist attitudes of the time, there are few documents that have information about African American music. However, historians have discovered enough writing from that time to provide a rough idea of the roots of modern black music.

# CHAPTER ONE
## BLACK MUSIC'S BEGINNINGS

Slaves were brought to the American colonies from Africa starting in the 1600s, and by the mid-1700s, they numbered around 200,000. They lived primarily in the South and were forced to labor on huge plantations that produced crops such as rice, tobacco, and cotton.

As white masters were enriched by their labor, slaves lived in terrible conditions and had no civil rights. They were regarded as property, not humans. Music based on African rhythms and religious faith helped slaves retain their humanity and hope for a future where they could live as free men and women.

### African Roots

Slaves brought to the American colonies came from several distinct groups. As such, their music reflected cultural differences. Broadly

*Hundreds of thousands of Africans were taken from their homes and forced to work on plantations similar to this one. Many used music to carry on African traditions.*

speaking, however, these groups all shared certain characteristics.

For example, vocal music was typically group singing. Generally, a solo vocalist alternated with an answering chorus, a style known today as call-and-response. Another shared element was the use of certain scales, such as the five-note pentatonic scale and using flatted notes, which today are called blue notes. A third major characteristic of African music was the use of polyrhythms—multiple, overlapping rhythms, such as 4/4 (four beats to a measure) played against 3/4 (three beats to a measure). These rhythms were played on drums, with sticks, and with body percussion, such as clapping.

These main characteristics of African music—call-and-response singing, certain scales and notes, and polyrhythms—would, in time, form the foundation of black American music. Indeed, they would influence music all over the world. Music historian Robert Darden commented: "Among the richest of the lavish gifts Africa has given to the world is rhythm. The beat. The sound of wood on wood, hand on hand. That indefinable pulse that sets blood to racing and toes to tapping."[3]

## The Universal Instrument

In Africa, singing, dancing, and drumming were crucial parts of life. Daily occurrences and major events alike were commemorated, or celebrated, with song. Late historian Eileen Southern wrote, "For almost every activity in the life of the individual or the community there was an appropriate music; it was an integral part of life from the hour of birth to beyond the grave."[4]

In America, slaves did their best to reproduce familiar music. They made instruments with whatever materials they could find, such as flutes made from lengths of cane. Occasionally, they also learned new styles; whites sometimes—though infrequently—taught slaves to play Western instruments, such as the violin or the fiddle.

However, slaves were commonly forbidden to play drums. In Africa, drummers could use their instruments to communicate over long distances. By banning drums, masters kept slaves on isolated plantations from planning rebellions with others. Despite this restriction, slaves always had one instrument with them: their voice. One of the common features across all of slave-owning America was the fact that slaves sang. As new generations grew up and African languages were forgotten, the songs of slaves were increasingly in English.

These songs reflected the African tradition of musical improvisation. African singers routinely put their own individual stamps on otherwise familiar songs, and slaves continued to use the technique. They altered old melodies and lyrics or invented entirely new songs. This sharply contrasted with European folk music traditions, which emphasized sticking as closely as possible to the original music.

The slaves sang for many reasons. A song might be used as a lullaby, a way to get through a hard day's work, a sad complaint, or a tune sung simply for pleasure. Sometimes, this pleasure involved making fun of owners; an observer in Maryland noted in 1774 that when they had a break from working, slaves amused themselves with "very [funny] music indeed," making up songs that portrayed their white masters "in a very satirical manner."[5]

## Religion in Music

Another important reason for singing was to express religious faith. The first slaves brought African religion with them, but they were also introduced to Christianity by white masters and later generations adopted the Christian faith as their own.

Although Christianity was forced on slaves in some cases, most willingly embraced it and became wholehearted believers. Christianity's promise of an afterlife offered hope and its declaration of the equality of people before God appealed to slaves. Furthermore, some Bible stories—Moses delivering the Jews from slavery, Jonah regaining freedom through faith—resonated powerfully with many slaves.

During worship services, African Americans and whites were generally kept separate, although sometimes they were allowed to worship together. For example, camp meetings—open-air events for preaching and singing—had both black and white congregations. A Swedish visitor attending a meeting in Georgia in the early 1800s noted: "A magnificent choir! Most likely the sound [came] from the black portion of the assembly, as their number was three times that of the whites, and their voices are naturally beautiful and pure."[6]

Over time, African religious music merged with European gospels and hymns. From this mixture, a large, varied, and mostly anonymously written body of songs developed. Songs once sung to ancestor spirits or African

*Though most aspects of early American life were segregated, some outdoor religious ceremonies, such as this one, had both blacks and whites worshipping together.*

and freedom from slavery. Eventually, some double meanings even contained coded messages that were associated with the Underground Railroad, the network of whites and free blacks that helped Southern slaves escape their masters. In "Follow the Drinking Gourd," a famous example, the drinking gourd was code for the Big Dipper constellation, and the song told escaping slaves to keep heading North, toward freedom:

gods were now sung to Jesus or Moses. Such songs eventually became known as spirituals. These powerful reflections of slave life were, as African American composer James Weldon Johnson described, "forged of sorrow in the heat of religious fervor."[7]

## Salvation and Freedom

Slaves radically changed the solemn, slow, and gloomy European hymns of the time. They embellished melodies by introducing melisma, a technique in which one syllable is stretched over several notes, and blue notes. They also added polyrhythms and freely changed lyrics.

The lyrics of spirituals frequently had double meanings, with images that evoked both religious salvation

*The river ends between two hills,*
*Follow the drinking gourd.*
*There's another river on the other side,*
*Follow the drinking gourd.*[8]

## New Churches After Slavery

The Underground Railroad was just one symbol of how slavery deeply divided the nation. After more than 100 years of black slavery, some white

# HOPE AND SADNESS IN SONG

Spirituals inspired hope, asked for forgiveness and freedom, and showcased a deep faith in achieving a better life. However, spirituals were also representative of a race that was abused and exploited. African American leader Frederick Douglass, remembering a childhood spent in slavery, wrote:

*Frederick Douglass was an outspoken opponent of slavery and an activist for African American rights. He was inspired to speak against slavery in part because of spirituals.*

*They told a tale which was then ... beyond my feeble comprehension; they were tones, loud, long, and deep, breathing the prayer and complaint of souls boiling over with the bitterest [suffering]. Every tone was a testimony against slavery, and a prayer to God for deliverance from chains... To those songs I trace my first... conceptions of the dehumanizing character of slavery.*[1]

1. Frederick Douglass, *My Bondage and My Freedom.* New York, NY: Miller, Orton & Mulligan, 1855, p. 99.

Americans realized how inhumane the practice was. A number of states, mainly northern, had abolished it by the early 1800s, but slavery flourished throughout the South. The issue came to a head when the Southern states seceded from the Union and the Civil War broke out in 1860.

In 1865, when the South was defeated in the bitter and bloody conflict, slavery was legally ended throughout the United States. Millions of newly freed slaves suddenly needed to enter mainstream American life. Because most were deeply religious, one result of this major social upheaval was the need for formal churches—something that previously had been denied to slaves.

The number of black churches across the South exploded, and each denomination started to develop its own style of music. Black churches in rural areas tended toward energetic, uninhibited singing and preaching. The music of urban congregations, such as the African Methodist Episcopal Church, was typically more calm and collected.

## Minstrel Shows

Prior to the Civil War, northern whites knew almost nothing about African American music. What little information they had came from racist minstrel shows. These were spectacles with white dancers, musicians, comedians, and singers who darkened their faces with blackface makeup and wore clothes that stereotyped African Americans. A large majority of minstrel performers were white, though some were black. The few African American performers also put on blackface makeup to make themselves as dark as possible.

Minstrel shows meant to give white audiences an entertaining view of plantation life. More importantly, they showed racially prejudiced white audiences the stereotypes they wanted to see: African Americans were cartoonish and not equal. Minstrel shows were wildly popular and dozens of performing troupes regularly toured North America and even internationally. One historian wrote, "For more than four decades … minstrelsy was the most popular form of theatrical entertainment in the United States and, to the rest of the world, America's unique contribution to the stage."[9]

From today's standpoint, minstrel shows are inappropriate and grotesquely racist. However, their importance in musical history cannot be ignored. Because they introduced black culture, even a false view of it, to white audiences, they were early instances of African American pop

# WIDESPREAD MINSTRELSY

Minstrel shows were prominent in American culture during the peak years of their popularity in the mid–19th century, and a small portion of their influence lingers even today. Writer Robert Cantwell said:

*The visual and linguistic coinage of the minstrelsy that has been circulating in America for a century and a half in thousands of forms beyond the stage itself: in sheet music, songbook and magazine covers, panoramas, popular lithographs, postcards, book jackets, scrapbooks, albums, catalogues, advertisements, product packaging, toys, as well as films, radio, television, folk festivals, and now even music videos. It is quite impossible even to think about "folklife" without [thinking of] the many motifs and images that descend from minstrelsy, which may be said to [be] bound up with questions of race and racial identity.*[1]

1. Robert Cantwell, *When We Were Good: The Folk Revival.* Cambridge, MA: Harvard University Press, 1996, p. 25.

music crossing racial and social barriers. Previously, whites had mostly listened to "white" music, blacks to "black" music. With the spread of minstrel shows, however, that was beginning to change.

## "Jimmy Crack Corn"

Minstrel shows introduced white audiences to several musical instruments with African origins. For instance, "the bones" were polished animal bones played as percussion instruments. The banjo was a stringed instrument from Africa that, over time, spread from slaves to become central to white folk music as well. The fiddle, long common to both white and black music, was another staple of the minstrel show.

Several types of songs were associated with minstrelsy. Some were folk tunes well-known in black communities, such as "Jimmy Crack Corn." Others were variations of familiar white folk melodies, such as "Turkey in the Straw." Professional songwriters wrote original minstrel songs that are still familiar today. Most of

# "THE WONDERFUL BEAUTY AND POWER OF OUR SONG"

Ella Sheppard was an early member of the Fisk Jubilee Singers, a group of talented African American singers from Fisk College. She reflected on her difficult experiences learning to sing slave spirituals:

*The slave songs ... were associated with slavery and the dark past, and represented things to be forgotten. Then, too, they were sacred to our parents who used them in their religious worship and shouted over them.*

*We finally grew willing to sing them privately ... we practiced softly, learning from each other the songs of our fathers. We did not dream of ever using them in public. Had Mr. White [director of the Fisk Jubilee Singers] suggested such a thing, we certainly [would have] rebelled.*

*After many months we began to appreciate the wonderful beauty and power of our song; but continued to sing in public the usual choruses, duets, solos, etc. Occasionally two or three slave songs were sung at the close of the concert. But the demand of the public changed this order. Soon the land rang with our slave songs.*[1]

1. Quoted in "Read what Fisk Jubilee Singer Ella Shepard wrote about spirituals." Tennessee4Me. Accessed February 28, 2017. www.tn4me.org/sapage.cfm/sa_id/52/era_id/5/major_id/6/minor_id/8/a_id/38.

these composers were white, such as Stephen Foster, whose songs include "Camptown Races" and "My Old Kentucky Home, Good Night." A handful of these composers were African American, such as James A. Bland, the originator of the popular "Oh! Dem Golden Slippers" and "Carry Me Back to Old Virginny."

## Youthful Voices Spread

A major turning point for black musicians came in the early 1870s with a dramatic surge of interest in spirituals

*Early banjos, such as this one, were relatively simple instruments. They were used in early African musical traditions. Today, the banjo is recognized around the world.*

among white northerners. A student singing group, the Fisk Jubilee Singers, from Fisk University in Nashville, Tennessee, inspired many Americans to explore this genre.

Organized as a fund-raising effort for the school, the Jubilee Singers first toured in 1871. Their performances of sentimental ballads and patriotic songs were skilled and dignified, but their nationwide tour was not well received until they added slave spirituals to their performances. The addition was suggested by the group's musical director, who was white, and the singers were reluctant at first. No former slave or descendant of one wanted to be reminded of that era.

However, the Jubilee Singers discovered that they could modify the traditional spirituals by smoothing their amateur style using European elements, such as piano accompaniment and classically performed harmonies. These adaptations struck a chord with audiences. The Jubilee Singers became a sensation, triumphantly singing for cheering crowds at home and European royalty abroad.

Within a few years, they earned enough money to build a six-story building that is still a centerpiece of Fisk University. Meanwhile, other African American groups sprang up to take advantage of the Jubilee Singers' popularity. There was also increased demand for spirituals in sheet music. In the days before recordings, radio, and the Internet, people enjoyed music by learning from sheet music. This was the first big break for African American musical genres.

## Steel-Driving Man

Another form of black popular music that developed in the late 1800s and early 1900s was the ballad, a type of secular (nonreligious) folk song. African American ballads were modeled on ancient British storytelling songs, part of the traditional music of many white settlers.

Black musicians incorporated African rhythms and vocal styles into the ballad format. They also wrote new lyrics and story lines. Standard ballads of the early 1800s involved white heroes and heroines, frequently lovers who experienced some kind of tragedy. African Americans, however, adapted the ballads to be more in tune with the experiences of black communities. Moreover, African Americans had their own set of folktales, with unique characters, and these black heroes and heroines were adapted into musical ballads.

A familiar example of the black folk ballad is "John Henry," a tall tale about a legendary steel-driving man who worked himself to death on the railroad. Another is "Stagger Lee," about a famous killer who was, in the words of historians, "so bad that the flies wouldn't even fly around his head in the summertime, and snow wouldn't fall on his house in the winter. He was bad."[10] Even though these ballad characters were not the most pure or noble people, they were considered heroes of African American folklore. Both John Henry and Stagger Lee were symbols of black resistance in a white-dominated world, and they showed up in song.

## A New Religious Movement

As the ballad form developed, African American religious music continued to undergo changes. One major shift came with the rise of Pentecostalism, which became widespread around the turn of the 20th century. Pentecostalism was hugely popular among both black and white Christians, and dozens of unique denominations developed within it. The largest black Pentecostal church, the Church of God in Christ, was created around 1900. The exact date of its founding is disputed by historians and members of the church, but everyone agrees that Charles H. Mason, its first preacher, was the most important member. It was hugely popular in the early 20th century. Today, membership is more than 6 million.

Pentecostal worship was more vocal and energetic than older religious traditions. Churchgoers spoke out during services, encouraging the preacher or testifying to their own faith. They shouted, fainted, or ran up and down the aisles as religious passion moved them.

Such passionate worship extended

to Pentecostal music. Group singing in services was more enthusiastic than that of older Christian denominations, and many churches added percussion as well. Music historian Horace Clarence Boyer noted that Pentecostal services were unique for their "forceful and jubilant singing, dramatic testimonies, hand clapping, foot stamping, and beating of drums, tambourines, and triangles (and pots, pans, and washboards when professional instruments were not available)."[11]

## Moving to the Industrial North

Though the Pentecostal movement was especially strong in rural areas, it also developed a powerful influence in cities. In part, this was because of a major shift in the nation's population in the early 1900s. During this period, huge numbers of African Americans left the South for the industrialized cities of the Midwest and Northeast. In the first few decades of the 1900s, African American populations in the largest U.S. cities went up by as much as 50 percent.

The new arrivals naturally brought their own musical traditions with them as they moved. Because cities were largely inhabited by white Americans, the spread of black musical traditions continued. During the next decades, African American popular music flourished, eventually developing into several important genres and moving steadily into mainstream American culture.

# CHAPTER TWO
## BRINGING
## A NEW ERA

The changing regional demographics of black America influenced the development of new music at the turn of the 20th century. Blacks born after the end of slavery moved to large cities in huge numbers looking for work in factories and a new way of life. Ragtime, blues, and jazz found their beginnings nationwide during this era. Moreover, with the emergence of new musical genres, many white Americans were increasingly open-minded with regard to listening to music produced by African Americans.

## A New Time

One musical tradition that emerged in the early 1900s was ragtime. The term "ragtime" refers to a specific rhythmic style—syncopation—that occurs when a normally unstressed musical beat is accented. Music historians David A. Jasen and Gene Jones called it "an ancient musical device, a trick that tickles the ear by putting a stress where we don't expect to hear it."[12]

The foundation of ragtime was laid during the slave era. Slaves altered traditional European dance music by syncopating it on banjos and fiddles. This was called "ragging" it. The origin of this term is unclear, but one theory is that people imagined the "cloth" of the music getting torn into rags when it was syncopated. Another idea is that ragtime is an abbreviation of "ragged time," meaning the tempo and feeling of syncopated music was ragged, or rough.

Minstrel shows were quick to adopt this catchy blend of African rhythm and European song, performing the earliest incarnations of ragtime music. There were also many ragtime guitarists, such as Blind Blake. By the late 1890s, however, the piano

*Skilled piano players typically created ragtime's unique rhythms. Many of the earliest innovators of this style were African American.*

A number of professional musicians focused on ragtime during its formative years. Music historians believe the first published ragtime piece was "Michigan Waters," written in 1892 by Tony Jackson, a composer from New Orleans, Louisiana. The following year, Fred Stone, a Detroit musician, was the first to use the word "ragtime" in a song title: "Ma Ragtime Baby." This new musical phenomenon was beginning to take off nationwide.

## Cakewalking Around the Country

Ragtime pianists were especially popular in the bar districts of midwestern and southern cities. Some were famous, such as New Orleans' legendary Jelly Roll Morton. Others were forgotten, despite having equally colorful names, such as Bad Hooks, Pluck Henry, Jack the Bear, and No Legs Cagey.

One man in particular became synonymous with ragtime. Scott Joplin, born in Texas, played piano in saloons across the Midwest and tried to sell sheet music of his original compositions. His success was modest until 1899, when he published "Maple Leaf Rag," named after a club in Sedalia,

was the instrument of choice. As the United States grew more prosperous and settled, pianos were increasingly common in saloons, clubs, and middle-class homes. They were the ideal instruments for ragtime's rhythms and harmonies. The left hand could pound out a steady beat while the right played intricate, syncopated ragtime melodies.

# LEGACY LEADS TO RAGTIME'S POPULARITY

In the later years of the 19th century, ragtime music exploded onto the musical scene. Inspired by slave music's adaptations of traditional European songs, it had the unique ability to bring African Americans and whites together. In this passage, musical historians Thomas L. Morgan and William Barlow reflected on the reasons for ragtime's popularity:

*Ragtime's complex historical legacy was perhaps a major reason for its widespread appeal among both blacks and whites. First and foremost, it was a dance music which drew on both European and African traditions. Second, ragtime was a style grounded in an ongoing, cross-cultural, racial parody: the slaves' parody of their masters ... In addition, ragtime was a rural folk music transposed to an urban and industrial context, where its machine-like rhythms became an expression of a lost innocence of bygone days and ways. And finally, as a novel popular music created by the first generation of African Americans born after slavery, ragtime represented an affirmation of their newly experienced freedoms and an optimistic vision of the future.*[1]

1. Thomas L. Morgan and William Barlow, *From Cakewalks to Concert Halls: An Illustrated History of African American Popular Music from 1895 to 1930*. Washington, DC: Elliott and Clark, 1992, p. 26.

Missouri, where Joplin lived for a few years. The catchy tune took the country by storm, reportedly selling more than 1 million copies of sheet music. By the turn of the 20th century, ragtime was a national fad.

From the beginning, ragtime and dance were closely joined. Writer James Weldon Johnson noted that ragtime "was music that demanded physical response, patting of the feet, drumming of the fingers, nodding of the head in time with the beat."[13] The biggest ragtime dance fad was the cakewalk, originally created by slaves as a parody of their masters.

*Scott Joplin was one of the most successful early ragtime musicians. Historians estimate that his famous "Maple Leaf Rag" sold more than 1 million copies.*

This dance involved men and women taking exaggerated, delicate steps in time with the syncopated music.

At the height of the ragtime craze, the cakewalk was so prevalent that dozens of regional dance contests were held, leading to a national Cakewalk Jubilee that was just as popular as the music that inspired it. One historian noted, "By the end of the century, the entertainment industry was sponsoring contests that offered two sets of prizes, one set for cakewalkers and the other set for ragtime pianists."[14]

## Ragtime and Blues

Even as ragtime swept the United States, a strikingly different musical style was taking shape. This new style, the blues, is one of the most enduring genres of all time. However, in the early 1900s, it was fighting against all the traditions of its biggest musical competitor. Ragtime was sophisticated, light, and refined; blues was rough, dark, and emotionally charged. Ragtime was mostly instrumental; the blues was vocal with instrumental accompaniment.

Ragtime was associated with wealth and the good life; the blues openly expressed a range of sad, or blue, emotions, and was sung and largely appreciated by poorer people. Nonetheless, many music historians consider the blues to be the essential foundation of future popular American music. According to one expert, "It is from the blues that all that may be called American music derives its most distinctive characteristics."[15]

These characteristics were built on a simple but sturdy framework, one that provided plenty of room for variation and improvisation. Each verse of a typical blues song had 12 measures in common 4/4 time. Originally, chord progressions, or the series of notes that come together to make melody, were fairly standard and did not vary. Lyrics, meanwhile, were catchy and repetitive—typically consisting of two repeated lines followed by a rhyming third line.

Like ragtime, the blues could be played on piano, but most early blues musicians used whatever easily obtained and easy-to-carry instruments they could find. These were mostly guitars, harmonicas, jugs to blow into, or basses made from washtubs and broomsticks. They devised ways to make these simple instruments sound fresh, such as sliding the neck of a bottle over metal guitar strings for an eerie, mournful sound.

## "A Boogie-Woogie Piano"

Blues singing, which is one of the most noticeable features that sets it apart from ragtime, was highly emotional. It alternated between terrifying, seductive, heartbreaking, or hilarious. Vocalists improvised freely on traditional song structures from other genres, borrowing the expressive bent notes, slurs, and shouts of the spirituals. These borrowed pieces emphasized the close connection between the blues and religious music.

Black religious music was also developing rapidly, and by the early decades of the 20th century, now being called gospel music, it was a highly stylized and unique genre in its own right. Gospel was not strictly popular music, because it was meant for worship and not general consumption. However, gospel was popular music in the sense that many people listened to and loved it. Furthermore, it deeply influenced other forms of popular music.

Gospel, which counted Mahalia Jackson and Sister Rosetta Tharpe among its greatest stars, was characterized by passionate vocals, large choirs, and unique instrumentation, such as a piano-organ combination. Its distinctive sound had a profound influence on the blues. As blues musician T-Bone Walker once remarked: "Of course, the blues come a lot from the church, too. The first I ever heard a boogie-woogie piano was the first time I went to church."[16]

## Origins of the Blues

The exact birth date of the blues is unknown. One anonymous blues musician once commented: "The blues? Ain't no first blues! The blues always been."[17] Despite a lack of concrete historical evidence, scholars generally agree that the blues had been developing for a number of years in the late 1890s and it was flowering by the 1920s.

The music's precise birthplace is equally hard to pinpoint, though many historians have concluded it was undoubtedly the South. Several regions developed distinct blues styles, notably Louisiana, East Texas, and the Piedmont area of North Carolina. The Mississippi Delta, however, is commonly considered the area where the blues initially developed. This largely agricultural region encompasses both sides of the Mississippi River and stretches roughly from Memphis, Tennessee, south to Natchez, Mississippi.

At the time, the Mississippi Delta was home to the nation's densest population of African Americans. This large, tight-knit community produced hundreds of performers who shaped the blues in its early decades. Many were obscure even in those times, playing only for drinks or meals in local bars or inns. Others, however, used their musical talents and ambition to gain fame that stretched from coast to coast.

## An Artistic Generation

During the early 20th century, the United States saw the rise of a new generation of talented, crowd-pleasing musicians. Among the many classic blues artists of this early period were pianists Albert Ammons, Pete Johnson, and Meade Lux Lewis, all of whom pioneered a fast-paced, lively subgenre of blues called boogie-woogie. Other prominent blues players were guitarist-singers Charley Patton, Son House, Blind Lemon Jefferson, and Skip James. Women also participated in the trending music. Singers Mamie Smith, Ma Rainey, and Bessie Smith all had an impact on early blues. These exceptional talents were all widely popular between the 1920s and 1940s, but the most influential original blues artist was Robert Johnson.

Johnson's haunting vocals and unrivaled skill with the guitar set a high standard, and his life's story formed the template for the stereotypical bluesman's life: hard drinking and fast living. As a young man in Robinsonville, Mississippi, Johnson met blues pioneers Patton and House; neither of these men were impressed with his musical ability. He reportedly then spent a year away from Robinsonville, and when he returned, he was an instant legend. The other musicians in the area had no idea how he transformed his music from bland to extraordinary in such a short space of time.

According to myth, Johnson made a deal with the devil: In return for his soul, he would be able to play

*Robert Johnson stunned both musicians and audiences with his incredibly skillful guitar playing. Though he acquired great fame, he died at a young age.*

and sing blues better than anyone else. The historical record shows that he was probably mentored by an amateur blues guitarist named Ike Zinneman. Moreover, as he traveled away from Robinsonville, historians believe he was exposed to different, innovative musical styles. He was able to combine his new teachings with the classic Mississippi Delta blues, which created an entirely new style. Regardless of how he acquired his talent, his glory was short-lived. Johnson, still in his twenties, was fatally poisoned in 1938.

Another crucial figure during this period was Memphis composer and bandleader W.C. Handy. Handy called himself the Father of the Blues, but he is most remembered not for pioneering the original blues genre but for popularizing it. According to legend, he heard a man singing the blues in a train station in 1903 and was inspired to convert what he heard into written music—apparently becoming the first to write down blues music. His later compositions, including the wildly popular "Memphis Blues" in 1912 and "St. Louis Blues" in 1914, smoothed the music's rough edges, making it more appealing to a white audience.

## Jazz Grows out of New Orleans

As the blues took on a definite shape and spread across America, another fundamental genre of African American–created music was developing. Much like blues, the exact history of jazz is uncertain, but it is generally accepted that the music was born in New Orleans, came North to Chicago, Illinois, by way of traveling musicians, then East to New York City—and from there, it spread around the world.

# MEMPHIS IN NEW YORK

At the turn of the 20th century, audiences began seeing the first large-scale black bands that were not based on minstrelsy tradition. These were influenced by more authentic African American genres and European concerts and musical styles. They combined traditional African instruments, such as the banjo, with traditional European concert-band instruments, such as trumpets.

One prominent group was the Memphis Students, formed in 1905 by Ernest Hogan, a stage performer, and Will Marion Cook, a violinist and classical composer. Despite their name, the Memphis Students were based in New York City. The group was a successful dance orchestra, backing powerful vocal soloists with a full orchestra of banjos, mandolins, guitars, saxophones, drums, violin, brass, and double bass.

New Orleans was a logical birthplace for the new style. As Louisiana's largest city, it has always been among America's most intensely musical towns with a rich mixture of French, Spanish, British, African, and Caribbean influences. Around the turn of the 20th century, New Orleans was an open-minded, fast-paced port town. Ragtime pianists flocked there for work in the bars, clubs, and saloons.

The city also had dozens of primarily African American brass bands, typically associated with social and benevolent societies. Performing at functions such as picnics, parades, and funerals, these bands combined traditional European marching music with black musical traditions.

## Jazz Musicians Absorbed Everything

Furthermore, the city featured many dance bands. Some were casual trios or quartets that played in simple halls for relatively small audiences. Others were larger orchestras that played more formal, ballroom-style music for refined dances. The earliest jazz musicians created a unique musical flavor that expanded and adapted alongside these and other trending genres, and eventually emerged as one of America's most famous genres: jazz.

New Orleans musicians played wherever they could, becoming fluent in all of these styles. They seemingly absorbed everything; out of this musical stew came the classic jazz sound. It incorporated ragtime, African rhythms, improvisation, and Latin rhythms imported from Cuba. A typical band was composed of a front line, generally a clarinet, trombone, and cornet or trumpet, supported by a rhythm section consisting of a guitar or banjo, piano, bass or tuba, and drums.

Unlike ragtime, which was played from a book of sheet music, jazz (or "jass," as it was called before the 1920s) emphasized improvisation. The ability to improvise was crucial, and jazz musicians looked down on those who could not improvise well. Playing from the heart with spontaneous emotion was, to them, a talent far superior to being able to read music from a sheet.

## Louis Armstrong

Several extremely talented musicians stand out among New Orleans' jazz pioneers. One was Charles "Buddy" Bolden, a brilliant cornet player with a famously loud, clear tone; according to legend, people could hear him from 10 miles (16 km) away if he played outside. Other outstanding New Orleans performers included Jelly Roll Morton, cornet player Joe "King" Oliver, trombonist Edward "Kid" Ory, and clarinet and soprano saxophone master Sidney Bechet.

Of all the incredible talent to arise from early New Orleans jazz, the most

*Louis Armstrong is one of the most famous musicians of all time. He revolutionized the way most people thought about music and he has influenced countless other artists.*

famous and influential was trumpet and cornet player (and sometimes singer) Louis Armstrong. Armstrong was an unrivaled genius, a bighearted individual, and undoubtedly one of the most important figures in jazz history. Many historians and artists consider him one of the greatest American musicians in any genre at any time.

Fondly called Satchmo, Armstrong burst onto the national scene in the 1920s with Kid Ory's Creole Jazz Band. Armstrong's first solo productions, commonly named the Hot Five and Hot Seven recordings, set unparalleled standards for imagination, technique, and sheer joy in playing. His overall influence is incalculable; as another genius of jazz, Miles Davis, once remarked, "You can't play anything on a horn that Louis hasn't played."[18]

## Replacing Minstrels

Jazz eventually absorbed ragtime as a popular style. Meanwhile, the once-popular minstrel shows and their racist stereotypes were dying and being replaced by musical theater. Though musical theater grew out of traditional white forms of entertainment in the early 1900s, African Americans in musical theater also prospered during the 1920s and 1930s.

One especially influential show was 1921's *Shuffle Along*, the first Broadway musical produced, created, and performed entirely by African Americans. It was so popular during its original Broadway run that it was able to expand outside New York City and the production went on a national tour in 1922. *Shuffle Along* introduced a number of hit songs, including "(I'm Just) Wild About Harry." It also launched three future stars: Florence Mills, Paul Robeson, and Josephine Baker. It broke new ground by depicting dignified, sophisticated, and intelligent African American characters—a far cry from the minstrel era of racist stereotypes.

Other outstanding productions included *Running Wild*, which launched a dance sensation called the Charleston in 1923. *Blackbirds of 1928* introduced Bill "Bojangles" Robinson, a performer who became the king of tap dancers. In 1929, *Hot Chocolates* featured the famous pianist, singer, and comedian Thomas "Fats" Waller performing some of his most famous compositions, including "Ain't Misbehavin'."

## African American Vaudevillians

Also on the rise was vaudeville. These shows were variety programs that featured everything from comedy and

# CHANGING LOVE

The musical *Shuffle Along*, which premiered in 1921, broke a number of important racial barriers. Until 1921, a serious romantic love scene between African Americans had never been shown onstage. The accepted belief was such scenes between black characters had to be comedic because white audiences would be uncomfortable with a serious one.

*Shuffle Along* changed that. At the premiere of the show, during a love scene between black characters, composer Eubie Blake was playing piano for the romantic ballad "Love Will Find a Way." Legend has it that other members of the production, however, were waiting anxiously by the exit, ready to flee if the white theater audience showed signs of violence. To their relief, the scene was well received, and another wall in the racial divide had crumbled.

singing to animal acts and dancers. Thanks to newly built rail lines across the country, vaudeville shows became so widespread that even the smallest town could see new acts every week. Two historians noted, "Vaudeville blanketed America as ... minstrel shows never had, reaching into towns large and small."[19]

For black vaudevillians, their main connection to the stage was through the Theater Owners Booking Association (TOBA), a string of theaters throughout the South, Midwest, and East. At its peak, TOBA had nearly 100 participating theaters and even more performers. For African American vaudevillians, playing TOBA shows was rough and the pay was poor. Some performers joked that the initials stood for "Tough on Black Artists." Still, it provided a way for African American artists to get on stage and earn a little money doing what they loved.

Occasionally, black vaudeville performers moved on to achieve wider stardom, such as the husband-and-wife comedians known as Butterbeans and Susie. Another successful African American vaudevillian was comic Bert Williams, of whom the African American activist Booker T. Washington once remarked: "He has done more for our race than I have. He has smiled his way into people's hearts; I have been obliged to fight my way."[20]

## Recording the Blues

Williams was one of many performers of the era who benefited from a new invention: the phonograph record. Since the earliest days of the technology, when recordings were made on fragile glass or wax cylinders, ragtime, blues, spirituals, and jazz had been recorded. However, professional recordings of black musicians remained rare, since record companies doubted they would sell.

A black entrepreneur and musician named Perry Bradford proved them wrong in 1920. Bradford convinced the Okeh record company to record Mamie Smith singing "Crazy Blues." It was a runaway success. Smith became one of the decade's most popular vocalists, and the way was paved for other African American musicians in the early 20th century.

The success of "Crazy Blues" inspired several companies to create divisions just for "race records." This was a term used for any recording that was produced or played primarily by African Americans. By 1925, hundreds of race records were appearing every year, and African Americans were buying five million copies annually.

Despite the good sales numbers, most of the black performers on these records received only a fraction of the money they earned for the record companies. Even the most successful recording artists, such as Bessie Smith, were unable to truly capitalize on their records' astounding sales. Nonetheless, the advent of race records considerably brightened the future for African American artists. Though they were not enriched directly from the sale of records, their names spread across the country and they could earn money by playing in front of large audiences.

## Music Sales Collapse

The good times did not last long, however. In 1929, a devastating economic crash, the Great Depression, created chaos across America. Millions of people were starving and had little money to spare for records, nightclubs, or theaters. Within a few years, the music industry collapsed almost entirely.

A number of vaudeville performing venues, including TOBA, went out of business. In the record industry, annual sales overall fell from $100 million in 1927 to $6 million in 1933. A race record could sell about ten thousand copies in the mid-1920s; by 1932, that average plummeted to just a few hundred.

Times were bleak, but some positive factors offset this grim picture.

Prohibition, the national ban on alcohol from 1920 to 1933, was a huge bonus for musicians because of the immediate rise in the number of speakeasies—illegal nightclubs—that needed live entertainment. The rising popularity of the jukebox also helped boost record sales. African American musicians also slowly began making progress to get their music on the radio, another recent invention that was quickly spreading into all corners of the nation.

Overall, by the mid-1930s, black popular music was truly cracking into mainstream American culture. Though some prejudice was still widespread, the worst stereotypes were disappearing. African American musicians and songwriters were being recognized as innovative and financially successful style-setters. The time was ripe for the next major development in African American music.

# CHAPTER THREE

# SWINGING
# AND BOPPING

The new genres of jazz music played a prominent role in the 1930s and early 1940s. Jazz diversified into regional varieties and developed into the widespread phenomenon of swing. Also called big band music, swing drew a large audience by embracing dance-like rhythms and catchy melodies. It was the high point of jazz's popularity.

## Swing's Big Bands

Two of the key figures in swing were Fletcher Henderson, a pianist and bandleader, and his gifted arranger, Don Redman. An arranger is similar to a composer; they decide when and how the various parts of a band or orchestra play. Henderson's orchestra, based in New York City, embodied the ways in which swing differed from its older cousin, the original New Orleans jazz.

One difference was size. In contrast to a typical New Orleans–style group of five or six musicians, a band like Henderson's had twice that or more. These players were grouped into three sections: rhythm (piano, guitar, bass, and drums), brass (trumpets and trombones), and reeds (saxophones and clarinets). The bandleader was typically the conductor and often played an instrument as well.

This enlarged size also caused a significant change in style. Bigger groups could not improvise simultaneously, as older jazz bands did, without creating musical chaos. To emphasize the ability of its members, swing groups allowed improvisation by soloists while the other musicians supported them with simple rhythms. These solos were balanced against written-out sections where the orchestra played as a single cohesive unit.

Another characteristic of swing is the contrast between brass and reed sections. These groups built excitement by creating call-and-response "battles," where one group would play an impressive solo, followed by the others trying to outdo them. Swing also featured singers more frequently and prominently than earlier styles. Swing created a new rhythmic standard as well: steady accents on all four beats, a flowing rhythm that largely replaced the two-beat rhythm of older jazz.

## Depression-Era Entertainment

The new style took hold just as the Depression was deepening in the mid-1930s. Dancing to a swing band was an inexpensive way to spend time, one that even the poor could afford. Hundreds of orchestras and ballrooms sprang up across the country to accommodate dancers looking for an affordable night out.

White musicians quickly jumped on the fad. Some white bandleaders, including Paul Whiteman, played watered-down, semi-orchestral swing, but Whiteman was considered too exaggerated for people who appreciated the origins of swing music. Others, such as Glenn Miller,

Artie Shaw, and Benny Goodman, led inventive and genuinely swinging bands. Goodman, sometimes called the King of Swing, was also a pioneer, directing racially integrated groups at a time when this was still controversial, as much of the country was still heavily segregated by race.

Competition was fierce between white and black bands alike, and the best ensembles got the most money. Among the major African American bandleaders, in addition to Fletcher Henderson, were Jimmie Lunceford, Earl "Fatha" Hines, Luis Russell, Chick Webb, and Cab Calloway. At the top, however, were two band-leading pianists with royal nicknames: Edward

*Benny Goodman helped increase the popularity of the African American–inspired swing style. He was also one of the first bandleaders to have a multiracial band.*

Ellington and William Basie, better known as the Duke and the Count.

## American Royalty

In New York City, the suave and talented Duke Ellington ruled. Ellington's crucial role in the history of jazz cannot be overstated. To many, he is second in importance only to Louis Armstrong. Author Albert Murray noted, "I don't think anybody has achieved a higher [artistic] synthesis of the American experience than Duke Ellington expressed in his music."[21]

Ellington stood out because of his

*One of America's most beloved swing musicians is Duke Ellington. He and his band created unique, bold, and powerful music for many years.*

brilliantly imaginative, highly sophisticated individual compositions and the outstanding musicians in his orchestra. To casual listeners at the time, all swing music often seemed to sound similar, no matter who wrote or who played it. Ellington's compositions, on the other hand, had a unique sound, and they were always custom-crafted for specific players in his band.

It was thus impossible to separate individual players from the Ellington sound. His piece "Warm Valley," for instance, needed the liquid, emotional tone of alto saxophonist Johnny Hodges to sound right. Jazz critic Whitney Balliett commented, "Most of the big bands ... came in two distinct parts—their leaders ... and the disposable hired [musicians]. But Ellington and his musicians were indivisible."[22]

The other giant of swing, Count Basie, made his reputation in Kansas City, Missouri. During the swing era, K.C., as Kansas City was known, was a booming rail center where gambling and drinking were openly tolerated, and the musicians who frequented the city's many clubs and bars developed their own distinctive swing out of this rough environment.

The K.C. sound was a robust genre built around simple, repeated musical figures called riffs. Its chief soloists were trumpeters and tenor saxophonists who were deeply influenced by the blues. Indeed, the blues was its cornerstone, one historian noted: "Blues could ... fit any mood; played fast, it generated excitement, and played slowly, it could be as [sad] as desired."[23]

Kansas City bands were collectively known as territory bands because they played a regular series of clubs around the Midwest and South. Though territory bands did a lot of playing in the these regions, their live performances rarely went eastward. These groups nonetheless produced some influential African American bandleaders, including Walter Page and Jay McShann.

The greatest and most influential musician to arise from these groups, however, was Basie. His juggernaut band was anchored by a rock-solid rhythm section featuring the leader's lean, elegant piano. Other featured soloists in his group were saxophonists Lester Young and Herschel Evans and trumpeter Buck Clayton. Basie's band featured a rotating group of singers, including such gifted performers as Billie Holiday, Joe Williams, and Jimmy Rushing.

## Playing Well with Others

The Ellington and Basie bands, big ensembles working together, exemplified the way in which swing was, first and foremost, a group effort. A number of gifted soloists also emerged during these years, distinguishing themselves from their swing bands. For example, the many outstanding pianists, in addition to Ellington and Basie, included Earl "Fatha" Hines, Teddy Wilson, and Art Tatum.

The tenor saxophone was not a common jazz instrument until the swing years, when soloists, including Coleman Hawkins and Ben Webster, made it a frontline instrument. Their powerful and passionate playing made the lesser-known brother to the alto saxophone a household name. Trumpet standouts included Harry "Sweets" Edison, Roy Eldridge, and Buck Clayton. Their improvisational powers showcased how beautiful the common instrument could sound.

Alongside instrumentalists, vocalists were also important to big bands. Typically, singers performed part of a song before stepping aside for other soloists, though they were also featured in sections that gave them greater prominence. Some singers were sweet and refined, while others were fire-breathing shouters. In any case, nearly every swing band had at least one good vocalist on hand. An exception was the Ellington orchestra, which rose to prominence mostly on the strength of its brilliant leader and his instrumentalists.

# THE COTTON CLUB

In 1927, Duke Ellington began the performance engagement that brought him to widespread fame: an extended stay at the Cotton Club in Harlem, the largely black neighborhood in upper Manhattan that was a center of African American cultural life. Harlem had some of the best nightclubs in the world, both during and after Prohibition, and the best of the best was the elegant Cotton Club. It was an exclusive New York hotspot with many wealthy and influential patrons.

The customers at the Cotton Club were almost completely white, though African Americans were allowed in if they were major celebrities. Nearly all the entertainers, however, were African American. They took part in elaborate floor shows featuring singers, dancers, comedians, and chorus girls in costumes that changed with every number. Duke Ellington spent a number of years performing there, as did some other prominent African American performers, including Cab Calloway. Many historians have identified the Cotton Club as a springboard from which these musicians launched their legendary careers.

## Supreme Songstresses

Three African American female singers in particular stood out during the swing years of 1930 to 1950. One was the spectacularly gifted Ella Fitzgerald. She won a talent contest as a teenager, joined Chick Webb's band, led it after Webb's death, and went on to experience great success in a long solo career. Fitzgerald was especially renowned for her ability to scat, or create long, wordless strings of instrumental-like improvisations.

Equally talented there was the honey-voiced Sarah Vaughan. A daughter of casual musicians, she began studying music at a young age. She immediately found she had a talent for it. Like Fitzgerald, Vaughan was blessed with flawless pitch, a beautiful tone, and a range of extraordinary size and quality. Also like Fitzgerald, she had a long career that stretched far beyond the swing years.

Billie Holiday, another sensational singer, differed sharply from Fitzgerald and Vaughan in musical style. Holiday had a limited range and rarely strayed far from the melody. However, she also had brilliant, pristine timing and an unforgettably bittersweet voice. It mirrored the difficulties and sadness

*Ella Fitzgerald pushed the boundaries of what an African American woman could do in the early 20th century. She was hugely famous, wealthy, and a popular public figure.*

the singer experienced in her life, projecting a deep sense of loneliness and yearning to her audiences just by using her voice.

## Bebop: A Lifestyle

Swing lasted through World War II, but, as with all musical genres, it was eventually replaced in popularity by a new style. When swing fell from favor, big bands could not survive. Most bandleaders had to trim their groups down to a traditional jazz size: just five or six performers. An exception was Ellington, who managed to keep his large group intact due to their extreme fame and talent.

The genre that emerged to take swing's place was called bebop, or bop. The name was a playful take on the music's short, accented rhythms. The style was so cutting edge in its early days that it had no name. Drummer Kenny Clarke recalled, "The music wasn't called bop [at first]. In fact, we had no name for the music. We called ourselves modern."[24]

Bebop was a radical departure from traditional jazz and blues. It was not just music—it was a lifestyle. Bop musicians and followers had a self-contained subculture that had new ways of talking, acting, and dressing. They used new slang terms, distanced themselves from established practices, and dressed in unique, bold styles. Bop was intellectual, urbanized, and extremely hip. Drugs, which had long been part of the jazz scene, now became even more closely connected with it. Heroin, in particular, claimed many victims among the boppers.

## Bop Grows

This new music primarily developed in New York City clubs. One of the most popular was Minton's, which was located in Harlem. Minton's frequently hosted after-hours jam sessions where exceptional musicians

# BILLIE HOLIDAY

Billie Holiday stood out as a musician, even among the incredibly gifted jazz singers of the era. This was not because of the range of her voice or her ability to improvise, but because her voice carried an extraordinary emotional punch. Music critic and biographer John Chilton noted:

*The timbre of her voice was completely individual, and her incredible sense of rhythm and intuitive knowledge of harmony enabled her to phrase songs in a unique way. She could reshape the bleakest melody into something that offered a vast range of emotions to her listeners; her artistry and timing gave her the ability to make poetry out of the most [boring] lyrics.*[1]

1. John Chilton, *Billie's Blues: The Billie Holiday Story*, 1933–1959. Briarcliff Manor, NY: Da Capo Press, 1957, p. 19

tried to outdo each other. In addition to Clarke, the house band included: trumpeter Dizzy Gillespie, pianist Thelonious Monk, guitarist Charlie Christian, and alto saxophonist Charlie Parker. Many others emerged as bop pioneers as well, among them saxophonists Dexter Gordon, John Coltrane, and Sonny Rollins; trumpeter Miles Davis; drummer Max Roach; bassist Charlie Mingus; and pianist Bud Powell.

Bop bands were commonly small groups: rhythm sections consisting of piano, bass, and drums backing a few saxophonists and brass players. Occasionally, other instruments, such as guitars or vibraphones, were used as well. Vocals were not as prominent as in blues and swing, though bebop did have such outstanding singers as Eddie Jefferson, King Pleasure, and Betty Carter.

The music's foundations were a bold departure from swing. Bebop's harsh style emphasized complex rhythms, difficult harmonies, and unusual keys and tempos. Its tunes were often originally composed, but boppers frequently reworked and modified existing songs until they were unrecognizable. For example, Parker's "Anthropology" adapted the basic structure of an earlier song,

# NO NAME TO THE GAME

One of the most influential musicians of the bebop era was trumpeter Dizzy Gillespie. In his book describing his musical career, he discussed the origins of the word "bebop":

*We played a lot of original tunes that didn't have titles. We just wrote an introduction and a first chorus. I'd say, "Dee-da-pa-da-n-de-bop . . ." and we'd go into it. People, when they'd wanna ask for one of those numbers and didn't know the name, would ask for bebop. And the press picked it up and started calling it bebop.*[1]

1. Dizzy Gillespie and Al Fraser, *To Be, or Not—to Bop.* New York, NY: Doubleday, 1979, p. 208.

*A truly talented trumpeter, Dizzy Gillespie was one of the most important figures in the bebop era.*

George Gershwin's "I Got Rhythm."

Bebop was a hard, aggressive, urbanized sound. It was in tune with an accelerated and increasingly industrialized post–World War II world. Gillespie recalled that bop was "fast and furious ... going this way and that way; it might've looked and sounded like [chaos], but it really wasn't."[25]

As a musical genre, bebop took itself rather seriously. What beboppers played was, to them, not simple dance music. It was serious art that required intent listening. Miles Davis personified this by deliberately turning his back onstage, distancing himself from his audience and drawing extra attention to the music itself.

Needless to say, not everyone liked the new style. For fans of older jazz, bebop seemed cold and difficult to follow, offering nothing beyond showy style. One New York newspaper critic asserted that boppers were nothing more than "a cult of beret-topped, chin-whiskered followers with flashy clothes and big, flowing bow ties."[26] Nonetheless, bop was on the cutting edge of jazz well into the 1950s and spawned many subgroups. These were as varied as hard bop, West Coast, cool, bossa nova, and more. Each had its own distinctive elements; for example, cool bop's sound was, as the name implies, detached and less emotional. Davis's minimalist solos demonstrated this; the silence between notes was as important and expressive as the notes themselves.

## Electrifying the Blues

Despite combining and adapting so many styles, bebop's defiant attitude condemned it to remain a smaller-scale genre. It lost the wide audience that swing once enjoyed, and jazz was no longer used as the music for light entertainment and dancing. That role was filled, at least partially, by blues—which itself was undergoing changes.

Until the mid-1940s, the blues had been acoustic folk music with roots in the rural South. That style did not die out, but a new form developed during the late 1940s and 1950s: electric blues, also called urban blues. As the name suggests, this style used a still-new technology—amplification of instruments—to change its sound radically.

This change mirrored social changes among African Americans. Throughout the 1930s and 1940s, millions of black southerners were moving to the heavily industrialized cities in the North, Midwest, and West. They moved northward to get a chance at a better life; discrimination in the South was still a very real thing, and the new industries were built primarily in the North. Among the migrant families were dozens of talented blues musicians.

These performers found that their music was easier to hear in crowded dance halls if they used full drum kits and electric bass guitars. Furthermore, amplifying guitars and harmonicas, which were common in the blues genre, gave the musicians a wide range of new sounds to play with. Formerly a relaxed style, the blues took on a driving, aggressive edge when amplified—one that appealed strongly to dance hall patrons.

## Blues from the Midwest

Regional blues styles developed in cities such as Memphis, which boasted a number of talented players, such as guitarist B.B. King, and Los Angeles, California, which counted another guitarist, Aaron "T-Bone" Walker, among its stars. The center for electric blues, however, was Chicago. The city's South Side, in particular, was the place to be for this exciting new music.

Pianist Otis Spann, harmonica player and singer Howlin' Wolf, and bassist Willie Dixon were just three of Chicago's most prominent blues musicians. There were a number of additional artists that had a lasting influence, but the undisputed king of Chicago blues was McKinley Morganfield. Better known as Muddy Waters, he was a singer, guitarist, and songwriter whose powerhouse bands always included the very best of Chicago's bluesmen.

A former tractor operator from Mississippi, Muddy Waters embodied the deep connections between the older acoustic blues and the exciting new electric blues style he helped create. His songs, including "I'm a Man" and "Mannish Boy," balance the laid-back ease of country blues with the gritty intensity of the electric version. He pioneered new ways of manipulating electric amplification to bring a unique sound to the blues.

## Record Sales Rise

Blues musicians and other black recording artists benefited from advances in recording technology during this mid-century period. This was a welcome change from the difficult war years. During that period, record sales had been low. This was partially because of the Great Depression in the late 1930s and partially because spending money was not as easy to come by during the war years.

In the years following World War II, the American economy was booming once again and record sales rose. In addition, several technological breakthroughs had been made. One was magnetic tape, which made the emergence of the tape recorder possible. Another was the long-playing (LP) record, which made it possible to record up to 30 minutes of material on 1 side of the record—a huge improvement over the previous limit of about 3 minutes.

Although the sales of singles were strong, artists were eager to exploit the new possibilities offered by the LP. For example, Miles Davis and a genius arranger, Gil Evans, recorded a series of extended records, including the now-classic *Sketches of Spain*. Recording these would have been impossible without the extended LP format.

In part because of the new LP's capabilities, record sales boomed in the 1950s for many African American artists. A prime example was Nat King Cole, who started his career as a bebop piano player but found lasting fame as a singer. As a pianist, Cole had only moderate success, but his remarkable voice sold millions of copies of hit songs. This made Cole not only the most successful black performer of his time, but also one of the most successful performers of any race or era.

## Progress

Cole's success indicated how far black popular music had come, and he was just one of many explosively successful African American musicians. Another sign was the rise of national jazz festivals, including famous events on both the East and West Coast. Furthermore, jazz was by now being taught in universities, and the American government was asking hugely popular black artists, such as Louis Armstrong, to serve as goodwill ambassadors overseas.

Black musicians had a long way to go before reaching anything like equality with their white counterparts, however. In record sales or any other measure of success, they were still not on equal footing in the dominantly white United States. Nonetheless, enormous strides had been made since the start of the century. The music that started as songs sung by slaves to pass the time had morphed and evolved into new genres. Jazz and blues had further changed over time, but the roots of swing and bebop still connected to centuries-old African traditions. As the middle and late 20th century years came along, even greater changes were about to come. The years after the war—the late 1940s and early 1950s—saw the development and emergence of a series of new, groundbreaking genres that would become major landmarks in American history.

# CHAPTER FOUR
# RHYTHM AND BLUES, ROCK AND ROLL

In the last years of the 1940s, *Billboard* editor Jerry Wexler was faced with a problem. A company that kept track of popular music in its famous charts, *Billboard* divided its statistics based on musical genres. However, up to 1947, they had lumped many of the various genres of largely African American popular music under just three prejudiced terms: Harlem Hit Parade, Sepia, and Race Music. Record companies did not like these names, and many other Americans believed they were demeaning and disrespectful. To fix this problem, Wexler came up with a new name that would not only stick, it would last for years to come: rhythm and blues.

R&B for short, this new genre was an engaging and lively combination of electric blues, gospel, and a saxophone-driven Midwest style of jazz. The sounds that came from this new genre were a culmination of years of African American musicianship. It seemed to be "liberated music ... it embodied the [passion] of gospel music, the throbbing vigor of boogie-woogie, the jump beat of swing, and the [difficulties] of life in the black ghetto."[27]

In the midcentury, R&B groups were typically small, cohesive groups. The rhythm section, which generally had electric guitar, piano, bass (either electric or string), and drums, was based on the standard electric blues band. They also included a saxophone and sometimes even a trumpet. The last piece, and arguably the most important, was the vocalist.

When the new genre was developing, the emphasis on R&B vocalists was mainly due to their gospel influences. Their voices were passionate, emotional, and often rough around the edges. Some of their vocal techniques were taken directly from gospel singing, including falsetto (extremely high-pitched singing) and melisma, spreading one word over multiple notes. Years later, Wexler commented, "If I understood then what I know now, I would have called it rhythm and gospel."[28]

## The Origins of R&B

R&B developed in several cities across the country, and the identity of the first true R&B artist is the source of ongoing debate among music historians. Texan Amos Milburn, Californians Saunders King and Roy Brown, and Nebraskan Wynonie Harris are just four of the many contenders that have a strong claim. The enormously energetic singer and saxophonist Louis Jordan, however, best represented the style's early years.

Jordan, born in Arkansas in 1908, was based in New York. He and his band, the Tympany Five, played a variety of material, from straightforward blues to commercial pop songs and territory band–style jump jazz. Jordan is best remembered, however, for witty tunes such as "Is You Is or Is You Ain't My Baby?" and "Ain't Nobody Here But Us Chickens."

Jordan's exciting attitude and unique material proved to be wildly popular. His records sold in the millions, and groups everywhere copied his style. Music historian Guthrie P. Ramsey Jr.

wrote: "Jordan's postwar rhythm and blues cast a long shadow of influence. It set the stage for a [major] movement that would dominate popular music in the following decades."[29]

Beyond Jordan's influence, distinctive R&B was stirring in a number of places. New Orleans, for example, continued to produce outstanding performers, such as the unique singer and pianist Professor Longhair. The Professor's musicianship was heavily laced with Cuban rhythms and other exotic influences. He enjoyed giving his bands colorful names, such as Professor Longhair and His Shuffling Hungarians.

Many cities, including New Orleans, New York, Chicago, Memphis, and Los Angeles, bred distinctive styles and performers. Los Angeles, for example, was home to many from the South and Southwest who had moved there in search of new jobs in the 1940s and 1950s. They liked territory-style jump blues and favored such performers as guitarist T-Bone Walker.

## New Ways to Listen

Radio, the newest technology of the midcentury, helped popularize R&B in its early days. Unique radio personalities, including Poppa Stoppa in New Orleans and Dewey Phillips in Memphis, featured the new genre

*When the radio spread into the homes of millions of Americans, musicians of all races were immediately given an instant popularity boost. Many black hosts and artists took advantage of this new technology.*

on their shows. While many pioneering R&B radio voices were white, a few were African American. The most prominent of these black hosts were Rufus Thomas and B.B. King—both based in Memphis, and both noted stage performers as well.

Dozens of independent record labels also helped spread the music. They were able to sign up-and-coming R&B bands because larger record companies mostly ignored the genre. R&B was thus almost exclusively distributed by smaller companies, such as Specialty (Los Angeles), Sun (Memphis), Atlantic (New York City), Ace (New Orleans), Savoy (Newark, New Jersey), Peacock (Houston, Texas), and Chess (Chicago).

These small companies were mostly regional, and limited in their ability to distribute records. Only a handful of R&B artists, such as Jordan, had national reputations. Most were local stars, trying to get work on regional dance circuits and making the occasional record. Guitarist Ike Turner, for instance, was a star around Memphis, but few people outside the region knew him. R&B as a whole did not take off until it evolved into something new: rock and roll.

## Rhythm to Rock, Blues to Roll

Like most new genres of music, the exact point of rock and roll's birth remains a topic of discussion among historians. They generally agree, however, that the shift was generational; rock and roll was music specifically for teenaged Americans. Its rebellious style strongly appealed to the younger generation, and since teenagers had increasing amounts of money to spend in the postwar years, rock music became big business.

# A FORTUNATE ACCIDENT

The song that many consider the first true rock-and-roll tune, Ike Turner's "Rocket 88," features a distinctive fuzzed-out sound from the band's lead guitarist. The story behind how that sound came to be illustrates the casual nature of pop record production in the early 1950s.

*Historical legend claims that guitarist Willie Kizart's amp fell off his car on the way to the studio, and one of the internal components was damaged. The band and producer Sam Phillips, later a legendary figure through his work with Elvis Presley, were too impatient to get it fixed. Phillips recalls, "It would probably have taken a couple of days [to fix it], so we started playing around with the ... thing. I stuffed a little paper in there ... and it sounded good ... And we decided to go ahead and record."*[1]

1. Quoted in Anthony DeCurtis, ed., *Present Tense: Rock & Roll and Culture.* Durham, NC: Duke University Press, 1992, p. 22.

In the late 1940s and early 1950s, several singers made recordings that were strong contenders for the title of first rock record. Among these were Roy Brown's "Good Rocking Tonight," Amos Milburn's "Chicken Shack Boogie," and Little Willie Littlefield's "K.C. Loving." Another likely candidate was "Rocket 88." This robust tune was recorded in Memphis in 1951 by Ike Turner's band, the Kings of Rhythm. With its grainy vocals, fuzzy guitar, and timeless lyrics about a fast car, "Rocket 88" clearly indicated rock and roll's musical direction and interests.

As had happened often before, white performers quickly picked up an originally African American trend. Their versions, usually less wild, appealed to wider audiences and thus were more successful financially. Rock and roll's first national hit—"Crazy Man Crazy" in 1953—was by a white musical group, Bill Haley and His Comets.

## Chuck Berry: Songwriting Genius

A tidal wave of performers—the first generation of rockers, white and black alike—followed Haley's success. Between 1953 and 1958, early rock's glory years, hundreds of potential stars fought for prominence. One—a teenager named Elvis Presley—would soon be the biggest of them all, at least financially. Among the others, three in particular stood out.

The first, Chuck Berry, is considered to be rock's true father by many historians and fans. As an aspiring bandleader in St. Louis, Berry achieved stardom with a style deeply influenced by Midwestern jump blues, characterized by driving, playful guitar riffs and performances that included his trademark duck walk.

*Chuck Berry was one of America's first rockers. His legacy is one of gifted musicianship and an innovative mind.*

Berry's genius, however, was in his songwriting. Among the composer's many tunes were "Maybellene," "Sweet Little Sixteen," "Johnny B. Goode," "The Promised Land," and "Roll Over Beethoven." Each was a model of verbal genius and wit, and they resonated deeply with the teenagers of the day. Berry's songs still inspire; according to one music critic, they are "a body of highly American imagery from which rock & roll continues to feed."[30] He passed away in 2017 at the age of 90.

## "Blueberry Hill"

Another outstanding early rocker was a product of New Orleans: Antoine "Fats" Domino. Of all the performers bred in the Big Easy during this period, none rose higher than Domino. He was already an experienced professional when rock and roll went national in the early 1950s. He had scored his first regional R&B hit ("The Fat Man") back in 1949, and he had been routinely producing successful popular music ever since.

Like many performers, Domino blurred the line between R&B and rock and roll, seeming to care little for genre distinctions. No matter what his music was called, Domino kept turning out hits. "Ain't That a Shame," "Blue Monday," "Blueberry Hill," and "Walkin' to New Orleans" were among the records he made that sold more than a million copies each.

Domino's cheerful personality, very different from the more bitter attitude typical of early rockers, was part of his appeal. The music was just as mild, blending a rolling piano with Domino's genial voice. It was a unique combination. New Orleans studio owner Cosimo Matassa said, "He could be singing the national anthem, you'd still know by the time he said two words it was him, obviously, unmistakably and pleasurably him."[31]

## Little Richard—Big Star

A third giant of the era hailed from Macon, Georgia: piano-thumping Richard Wayne Penniman, better known as Little Richard. He may not have been the most talented raw musician of the early rockers, but he was one of the wildest. No one had more attitude than Little Richard.

Richard's stage persona was built around his outrageous looks: towering hairdo, heavy makeup, and flamboyant wardrobe. Musically, his sound paired his emotional, gospel-influenced voice with his band's rugged musicianship. Then there were his nonsense lyrics, which were mostly just there to give texture to the surrounding music. Little Richard's biggest hits included "Tutti Frutti," "Long Tall Sally," and "Good Golly Miss Molly," and they made him hugely successful. Despite this, Richard, who was raised to be devoutly religious, was constantly torn between his deep faith and the temptations of a performer's wild lifestyle. At the peak of his career, the singer abandoned music for Bible study, though afterward he periodically returned to a life of rock and roll.

## Another New Genre

While Little Richard and others developed and polished the new rock and roll, others favored more traditional genres. One development was called doo-wop, a style of mostly unaccompanied vocal music. Doo-wop was born in the 1950s, when teenagers in cities such as New York and Philadelphia, Pennsylvania, gathered on street corners to sing. Instruments were rare, so they made music with just their voices.

Doo-wop was a nonreligious version of the male quartet style, a major form of gospel singing. These quartets often had five or six members, despite the name. Typically, a gospel quartet sang repeated phrases or nonsense syllables, harmonizing behind a lead vocalist's improvisations. Contrast was created through occasional solos by a falsetto singer or a deep, rumbling bass voice.

Like some gospel quartets, doo-wop groups occasionally used instrumental backing, but the emphasis remained on a cappella (unaccompanied) vocals. Highly musical group singing similar to this had already reached mainstream pop in the form of smooth groups such as the Ink Spots and the Mills Brothers. With doo-wop, it expanded into the less polished world of music that appealed to the nation's teens.

## Dominoes and Drifters

Classic doo-wop songs included "Goodnight, Sweetheart, Goodnight" by the Spaniels, "Earth Angel" by the Penguins, and "Crying in the Chapel" by the Orioles. Other prominent doo-woppers were named after birds, such as Ravens, Penguins, Robins, Flamingoes, and Falcons; cars, such as Cadillacs, Lincolns, El Dorados, and Impalas; and romantic images, such as Moonglows, Hearts, Charms, Heartbeats, and Dream Lovers.

Several outstanding singers emerged from doo-wop as solo stars. One was sweet-voiced Clyde McPhatter, who first came to fame with Billy Ward and the Dominoes, then formed his own group, the Drifters, before going solo. Among McPhatter's many hits were "Money Honey" and a confident new adaptation of the old holiday classic, "White Christmas."

Another star was the soulful Ben E. King, who also sang with the Drifters before going solo. King's many classics include "Save the Last Dance for Me," "Spanish Harlem," and "Stand by Me." A third major figure was Jackie Wilson, also a former member of the Dominoes. Wilson's dramatic voice and electrifying stage presence immortalized such songs as "Higher and Higher" and "Lonely Teardrops."

*As a member of Billy Ward and the Dominoes, Clyde McPhatter (middle) rose to fame for his unique and powerful voice. He became a national star when he formed his own group, the Drifters, shown here.*

# HOWLING RIGHT
# IN THE LIVING ROOM

Part of the success of R&B and its younger sibling, rock and roll, was due to the rise of radio shows specializing in the genre. A number of radio hosts, both black and white, helped introduce the music to a broader audience.

Among them were Dewey Phillips in Memphis and Bob Smith, better known as Wolfman Jack, whose gravelly voice was broadcast from a station just across the Mexican border. One especially influential station was WLAC in Nashville. Thanks to the station's powerful 50,000-watt signal, its nighttime R&B show could be heard throughout much of the eastern half of the United States.

The most prominent rock and roll radio personality was a white host named Alan Freed, sometimes called Moondog. In 1951, Freed began hosting a Cleveland radio show, primarily for white audiences, called *Moondog's Rock 'n' Roll Party*. The term "rock 'n' roll" or its variants had been used in the black community for years, both as a slang term and a musical style, but Freed was the first to use it with mainstream white audiences. His energetic on-air behavior fit the music he played. He howled like a wolf and beat his fist in time to the music in front of a microphone. He is widely credited for exposing white Americans to the rock and roll music of African Americans.

## Girl Groups Ruled

The female equivalents to doo-wop singers were called girl groups. They were relatively rare in the mid-1950s, when doo-wop was strong, but girl groups began to dominate in the late 1950s. By the early 1960s, they were among the most successful of all doo-wop or similar groups.

Like their male counterparts, girl groups specialized in close harmonies. One big difference was that they did not sing a cappella, partially because the groups did not have a deep bass voice to provide a strong bottom for their sound. Instead, small combos or orchestras backed them.

Among the most prominent girl groups were the Chiffons, Chantels, Dixie Cups, Crystals, Ronettes, Toys, and Shangri-Las. One of the top groups was the Shirelles, whose powerful and popular 1960 recording of "Will You Love Me Tomorrow?"

became the first number-one song by a girl group. This unprecedented hit was typical of the romantic love songs performed by girl groups. Others included "He's So Fine" by the Chiffons and "Chapel of Love" by the Dixie Cups. However, not all girl groups focused on romance. Some were edgier, focusing on creating a "bad girl" image for themselves.

## The Building of a Commercial Sound

Inevitably, doo-woppers and girl groups caught the attention of the commercial music industry. Music made especially for teenagers was becoming a big business, and the large record companies were moving in. They needed huge volumes of teen music to sell, and this led to the creation of a large pool of professional songwriters, music publishers, and producers headquartered in New York City's Brill Building.

They developed a style so recognizable that music historians often refer to it as the Brill Building Sound. Some of these

records were mediocre, grinding out material to make a fast buck; others were remarkably composed and well received. Unlike most doo-wop and girl group singers who performed their material, the Brill Building's employees were primarily white. These white workers wrote, produced, and published the music that black groups performed.

Among those associated with the Brill Building were Jerry Leiber and Mike Stoller, who wrote and produced tunes such as "Hound Dog," "Yakety Yak," and "Jailhouse Rock." Another prominent team was Mort Shuman and Doc Pomus, whose songs were typically emotionally

*This is the exterior of New York City's famous Brill Building. The recording studios here in the mid–20th century helped advance African American music and the music industry in general.*

complex. One of their most famous songs was "Save the Last Dance for Me," performed by the Drifters. Another Pomus-Shuman song, "A Teenager in Love," was so popular that at one point, three different versions, played by three different bands, appeared simultaneously on top sales charts in England.

Still another memorable partnership was the husband and wife team of Gerry Goffin and Carole King. They produced dozens of enduring and wildly success-ful hits, including "Up on the Roof," "Will You Love Me Tomorrow?" and "The Loco-Motion," which was record-ed by the pair's babysitter, Little Eva.

## Variety

Teenaged singers associated with the Brill Building were by no means the only African American pop perform-ers during this period; older musi-cians were still going strong. Powerful R&B and blues singers, such as Ruth Brown, Lavern Baker, and Big Joe Turner, remained popular. Smooth pop crooners, such as Charles Brown and Nat King Cole, also maintained substantial audiences. A blind and incredibly talented man named Ray Charles was just starting to enter into the public eye.

In short, there was plenty of music to choose from. Rising right alongside the emerging genres was the American teenager's interest in finding new music. They had money to spend and were interested in exploring their new freedoms. They embraced many of the new genres, and ever since the 1950s, they have been the trendsetters for upcoming music. Record companies discovered this in the midcentury and tried to get a diverse cast of musicians signed to release a huge variety of new music.

All this variety created new pos-sibilities for innovation. The 1960s were a decade of extraordinary social and political upheavals, and African American popular music rose to meet the challenge. It was about to enter a major new phase, as a new style—soul music—came to the forefront.

# CHAPTER FIVE

# MUSIC FOR THE SOUL

Going into the 1960s, black society found identity through the emerging Motown movement and other soul music from different corners of America. At the same time, music production techniques developed rapidly, allowing for more experimental and unique instrumentation and arrangement. By taking more intimate control of production, this allowed artists to express themselves in original ways and find a new space for social commentary.

## Music for a Movement

Previously, pop music of any genre had rarely been more than simple entertainment. It was for dancing, having a good time, or helping listeners forget their troubles. In the 1960s, however, African American pop music gained a social conscience because the music was closely influenced by a major event in American history. This was the civil rights movement, in which black citizens struggled for equality in such areas

*The March on Washington, shown here, was just one event of the civil rights movement. Black musicians used their art as a way of expressing the anger, fear, and hope that millions of Americans were feeling.*

as voting rights, job opportunities, and education.

Racial tensions ran high during this period, and pop songs reflected the uneasy mood. They increasingly addressed powerful and personal issues of civil rights as well as a related self-esteem movement that emphasized black pride. *Billboard* called such songs "music with a philosophy ... black nationalism in pop."[32]

As did most African American pop music that came before it, soul mixed sadness with joy. The civil rights movement had deep difficulties, serious disappointments, and very real battles. The feeling of soul was often positive, reflecting the hopeful nature of the struggle while still acknowledging that the struggle was real. One music scholar described this optimistic struggle:

> [Soul] was a peculiarly good-hearted and optimistic sort of music, and it is no accident that its popularity was limited to the early and middle Sixties, a time when awakening black pride went hand in hand with civil rights activism and racial progress seemed more real than [ever].[33]

## "I'm Black and I'm Proud"

Many soul songs directly reflected civil rights issues. One was James Brown's "Say It Loud—I'm Black and I'm Proud." Other examples included Curtis Mayfield and the Impressions' "We're a Winner" and "Keep On Pushing," Aretha Franklin's "Young, Gifted, and Black," and Sam Cooke's "A Change Is Gonna Come."

Civil rights activists also adopted and adapted a number of old gospel songs for their cause. The connection between the movement and traditional gospel was natural. Civil rights activism was intimately connected with the African American religious community; both shared common themes of freedom, equality, unity, and peace, and many key civil rights leaders were also ministers.

Old spirituals, outfitted with new words, were called freedom songs. Among the best known were "We Shall Overcome" and "Kumbaya." Such songs did a lot to lift the spirits of activists when they faced difficult times. The movement's most prominent leader, Martin Luther King Jr., noted that the songs provided "new courage and a sense of unity ... They keep alive a faith, a radiant hope in the future, particularly in our most [difficult] hours."[34]

## The Genius of Soul

Despite its deep connections to the civil rights movement, soul music was not just serious music about racial equality. Much of it—and some of the best—covered the same topics that popular music had always covered: dancing and romancing, having a good time, and expressing personal sadness or joy through song.

One performer in particular rarely spoke out publicly on political issues, but he was nonetheless one of the famous masters of the soul genre. This man was Ray Charles, sometimes simply called the Genius. Charles was a remarkable composer, pianist, and arranger, but the essence of his talent was his dazzling voice. Jazz critic Whitney Balliett noted:

> *Charles can sing anything short of lieder [German art songs] and opera ... He can shape his baritone voice into dark, shouting blocks of sound, reduce it to a goose-pimpling whisper, sing in a pure falsetto, yodel, resemble Nat Cole at his creamiest, and growl and rasp. He is always surprising.*[35]

Blind since he was a child in Florida, Charles was a professional musician by age 15 and spent years on the road before achieving fame. Early on, he was a smooth pop crooner who idolized singers like Nat King Cole. He found his own unique voice in the mid-1950s, when Atlantic Records executives encouraged an original style that combined his earthy vocals with rolling, gospel-influenced piano and a punchy, powerful horn section.

Charles's combination of religious and popular music, shocking at the time, was not new. He was considered the Genius because he did it more overtly, and better, than anyone else. Many of his songs were adapted from

*Ray Charles was an influential musician when he first emerged in the 1950s. He went on to perform countless classic hits.*

existing gospel songs; for example, "This Little Girl of Mine" started as "This Little Light of Mine." Charles scandalized many listeners, but he also perfectly expressed a recurring theme in soul music: the link between religious passion and romantic joy.

Charles first hit it big with "I've Got a Woman" and followed it with many others, including "Hallelujah I Love Her So" and "What'd I Say." His songs changed the course of soul by establishing a gold standard of quality. Writer Joe Levy said, "The hit records [Charles] made for Atlantic in the mid-50s mapped out everything that would happen to ... soul music in the years that followed."[36]

## Crossing Over from Gospel

The ones most scandalized by Charles's mix of religious and romantic passion were performers and fans of pure gospel music. Many of these people banned nonreligious song—sometimes called the "devil's music"—from their homes and flatly refused to perform it. Talented gospel singer Shirley Caesar once said, "The U.S.A. doesn't have enough money to make me sing rock'n'roll!"[37]

For many other singers and performers, however, the money and fame that pop music could bring were tempting.

Some artists viewed Charles, whose mix of sacred music with pop made him a rich celebrity, with envy. In the late 1950s, the appeal of wealth, fame, and a wider audience caused an established gospel star to cross over. His name was Sam Cooke.

Sam Cooke grew up in Chicago, the center of gospel music. As a teenager, he became the lead singer for one of gospel's top groups, the Soul Stirrers. Blessed with a soaring voice, movie-star looks, and a charismatic stage presence, he became sacred music's first young idol. Night after night, Cooke packed auditoriums, drove audiences wild with joy, and in particular made female fans fall in love. Fellow singer Wilson Pickett admiringly noted, "Them sisters fell out like dominoes when Sam took the lead. Bang. Flat-out. Piled three deep in the aisles."[38]

Cooke had ambitions far beyond gospel. He had always loved jazz and blues, though he had to listen to them secretly because of his highly religious, disapproving family. He took the plunge into pop and hit it big in 1957 with "You Send Me." The gospel community was devastated, but millions of others loved his new direction. Cooke followed "You Send Me" with more smash hits, including "Cupid," "Bring It On Home to Me," "Wonderful World," and "Havin' a Party." Some critics have noted he was exceptionally successful because he wrote most of his own music.

Others, following Cooke's example, at least partly abandoned gospel for careers in the emerging popular soul genre. In addition to Pickett, they included such stellar performers as Johnny Adams, Lou Rawls, Dinah Washington, and Irma Thomas.

## New Royalty

All of these new stars were extremely talented, but perhaps the most gifted of all was Aretha Franklin. Even in such a crowded and competitive field, Franklin's voice was without parallel. She fully earned her nicknames: Lady Soul and the Queen of Soul.

Franklin was born into religious royalty; her father, Reverend C.L. Franklin, was a minister in Detroit with a national reputation for his stirring sermons, and as a child, Aretha sang in his choir. Her first attempts at recording pop failed, but then Atlantic Records, as it had with Ray Charles, encouraged her to get in touch with her gospel roots. Franklin's producer, Jerry Wexler—the same man who coined the phrase "rhythm and blues"—recalls that his recording method was simple: "I took her to church, sat her down at the piano, and let her be herself."[39]

*One of the most recognizable voices and figures in American music history is Aretha Franklin. Her talent was exceptional, even during an era of impressive musicianship nationwide.*

The results paid off brilliantly. In 1967, Franklin's first Atlantic single, "I Never Loved a Man (the Way I Love You)," sold a million copies within weeks. She followed up this success with "Respect," "Chain of Fools," "(You Make Me Feel Like) A Natural Woman," and "Do Right Woman, Do Right Man." Each was marked by Franklin's hair-raising, powerfully honest voice; historian and author Peter Guralnick asserted, "There has been no pop singer more inspired than Aretha when it comes to sheer vocal artistry."[40]

## The Hardest-Working Man in Show Business

Another key individual in the birth of soul was James Brown—also known as the Hardest-Working Man in Show Business, Mr. Dynamite, and the Godfather of Soul. Brown's music was an unlikely hit; his voice was abrasive and gritty, the opposite of the standard, smooth commercial sound. His chief contribution to music was not his voice, but his brilliant use of rhythm. He quickly became both a star and an icon.

Brown had a difficult childhood in Georgia. Born in 1933, he lived with his great-aunt starting in 1938 after his parents divorced. Growing up in the racially discriminatory South during the Great Depression caused him to drift into a life of crime, and he was imprisoned at the age of 15 for attempted car theft. After his release, he joined a gospel quartet that became an R&B group called the Flames. Little Richard discovered the group, and James Brown soon rose to the level of superstar.

Brown's work was immediately successful, and his first record, "Please, Please, Please," sold 3 million copies. His sound was renowned for laying down extended, tight, polyrhythmic grooves. The melodies that flowed throughout Brown's songs were not very complex or technically difficult. His work depended mostly on rhythm for its forward movement.

Virtually every instrument in his bands became percussion. Guitars scratched out rhythms, horns provided rapid-fire bursts, and basses stressed the first beat of each measure. Over this carpet of rhythm, Brown's singing, grunts, moans, and shouts soared with a passionate fire.

*With his electrifying dancing, unique vocal skills, and powerful musical touch, James Brown became one of the biggest stars of the 20th century.*

# WEAVING THE RHYTHM

In James Brown's powerful band, as in traditional African music, rhythm was the musical foundation. The members of his groups learned to watch carefully for subtle hand and body gestures from their leader, which signaled rhythmic changes. According to Brown's longtime road manager, Alan Leeds, the total effect of this careful study was a complex musical patchwork: "So the magic became something like putting a quilt together—taking all the rhythm patterns and weaving them in such a magical way as to create this wonderful *feel* that's going to drive audiences crazy."[1]

1. Quoted in Robert Palmer, *Rock and Roll: An Unruly History*. New York, NY: Harmony, 1995, p. 243.

He was also well known for his electrifying dancing onstage, which was as precise and intense as his singing. According to legend, Brown sweat away seven pounds at every show.

His many hit singles included "I Got You (I Feel Good)," "Night Train," and "Papa's Got a Brand New Bag." However, Brown's extended grooves were not well suited to the early three-minute records. His true magic came out through live shows, and live recordings were best captured on LPs. One of these, 1963's *Live at the Apollo*, spent an unprecedented 66 weeks on the Billboard chart. Brown's fame increased over the years, and by 1971, he was among the highest-paid black entertainers in the world.

## Motor City Magic

Individuals like Brown were not the only musicians to forge unique, signature sounds. During the soul years of the 1960s, two record labels, Motown and Stax, stood out by becoming brand names that signed artists who produced distinctive, exciting sounds.

Motown Records was named for the location of its headquarters: Detroit, Michigan, the Motor City. Founded as a small operation in 1959 by Berry Gordy, Motown became one of the most successful black-owned music organizations in history. Along the way, not coincidentally, it made some unforgettable pop music. Gordy was fortunate in his choice of musical partners: William "Smokey" Robinson, a songwriter, producer, and the lead singer of the Miracles, was one of his first discoveries. Robinson's creamy voice melted hearts, and his brilliantly simple songs led Bob Dylan to call him "America's greatest living poet."[41]

Together with a gifted crew of associates, Gordy and Robinson created the signature Motown sound. Its catchy melodies, danceable beats, simple lyrics, and strong vocals were carefully crafted to be instantly recognizable to a broad range of listeners, even on low-quality car radios or transistor radios. As the legendary pop producer Phil Spector once remarked, "You put on a Motown record and it jumps at you."[42]

## Hit Song After Hit Song

Inspired by the efficiency of Detroit's automobile factories, Gordy created an assembly line for his performers, with different professionals performing specific functions at every step. An in-house band created the backing music. Experts crafted stage outfits and dance steps. Accountants kept careful control of money, paying out modest allowances to performers. There was even a charm school, where singers learned to act with grace, both on- and offstage.

The results of this detail-oriented work were immediate and stunning. Even before the company's operations were finalized, the hits started coming. One historian noted, "Motown put six records at the top of the pop charts before its bookkeepers had a systematic way of accounting for all the money it routinely advanced to the singers who made them."[43]

Not every Motown release was a groundbreaking hit, but its overall success rate was amazing. During the 1960s, the company sold millions of dollars worth of records every year. Among its most consistent stars were the Miracles, the Marvelettes, Marvin Gaye, Mary Wells, Martha and the Vandellas, and the Temptations. A blind child prodigy, Stevie Wonder, had his first hits during this period, while Diana Ross and the Supremes scored an astonishing 10 hit records within just 3 years.

## Another New Sound

In 1960, halfway across the country, a very different but equally influential label was developing in Memphis. This southern city already had a long history as a center for blues and R&B. Now it nurtured one of the most exciting subgenres of soul: the tough, earthy sounds of Stax. Like Motown, Stax was a consistently high-quality record label, with a number of highly successful recording artists.

Also like Motown, Stax began as a small company, operating as a small group of professionals out

# A MUSICAL FAMILY

Motown Records artists were kept on strict allowances, with the company paying out only a small portion of their earnings and keeping the rest in secured accounts, forcing the musicians to be responsible spenders. In return, company president Berry Gordy expected achievement, hard work, trust, and loyalty. To a great extent, that is what he got. Many recording artists who experienced success at Motown felt like they were part of a family. Because it started as a small, tight-knit company, its highest executives, including Gordy himself, believed that the company should operate in a welcoming environment.

of an old movie theater. Another similarity was its regular stable of gifted in-house producers, writers, singers, and musicians. Unlike Motown, however, Stax was a notably biracial organization—an unusual arrangement during this period of intense racial division nationwide. The label's top owners were white, while its producers, engineers, and musicians were racially mixed. Among its most frequently used backing musicians were Booker T. and the MGs and the Memphis Horns; both groups were multiracial.

## "In So Few Words"

Stax's featured artists, meanwhile, were primarily African American, each possessing a distinctive voice and style. Among the most successful were Sam and Dave, Carla Thomas, and Wilson Pickett. Stax was also home to the influential musician Otis Redding, whose voice blended the silky charm of Sam Cooke with the raspy urgency of James Brown.

Redding was also a gifted songwriter, responsible for such hits as "Respect" (famously recorded by Aretha Franklin), "I've Been Loving You Too Long (to Stop Now)," and "(Sittin' on) The Dock of the Bay." His career tragically ended in 1967 when he and several band members died in a plane crash. He was only 26 years old. MGs guitarist Steve Cropper summed up Redding's appeal: "He gets over to the people what he's talking about, and he does it in so few words that if you read them on paper they might not make any sense. But when you hear the way he sings them, you know exactly what he is talking about."[44]

## An Invasion Helps Revive the Blues

The powerful and unique singers of Stax and Motown—and countless other soul artists—defined the bulk of African American pop music in the early and mid-1960s. The blues, despite its popularity in previous decades, was generally ignored. However, after the Beatles emerged as a dominant musical force in the 1960s, a wave of English pop musicians swept the United States. This movement was called the British Invasion.

The Invasion bands commonly modeled themselves after African American blues and R&B artists. The Rolling Stones named themselves after a song by Muddy Waters. Pete Townshend, the Who's guitarist, idolized Steve Cropper. The Beatles were devoted fans of Fats Domino and Chuck Berry. The early years of blues and R&B had not only influenced the United States, but that powerful music had also traveled worldwide. When the British Invasion movement spread during the 1960s, Americans of all races rediscovered their love of these genres.

Most of these bands, suddenly famous among teenaged whites, were happy to acknowledge their musical debt to black America. This sparked a resurgence of interest in the blues; Muddy Waters and Howlin' Wolf were among the performers whose careers were boosted by the Invasion. Many African Americans were upset that white musicians, such as the Beatles, were once again getting most of the spotlight. Nonetheless, the attention from overseas did a lot to revive a classic form of traditionally African American music.

## Conflicts End an Era

The blues revival and the soul movement did not last. In particular, the end of soul's massive popularity was tied to that of the civil rights movement. The main period of that movement ended, in the opinion of many historians, with the assassination of Martin Luther King Jr. in 1968. Not coincidentally, classic soul music began to decrease in popularity around the same time.

The next period—the late 1960s and 1970s—was as uneasy and uncertain in America as the civil rights era had been. It was a different time, however—less optimistic and more conflicted. The course of black music reflected this uncertainty; the musical foundations were changing yet again.

# CHAPTER SIX
## MOVING AND GROOVING INTO THE SEVENTIES

Through the late 1960s and the 1970s, social and political upheaval in American society around Vietnam War protests and the civil rights movement were reflected in pop music. African American music gave listeners both social consciousness and a way to escape the tension of the real world. These musical trends took root in the late 1960s and would be ever-present in black music's future.

### The Jimi Hendrix Experience

One major black musician of the late 1960s and early 1970s was, conflictingly, actually associated with white music. By this time, rock and roll had become simply rock. It was the dominant form of popular music in the world, listened to globally by white teens and young adults. Only a handful of African American musicians of the era were true rockers. It can be argued that black music came into contact with rock in only one place during this period: the musicianship of Jimi Hendrix.

Born and raised in Seattle, Washington, Hendrix started his career as a blues and R&B guitarist with Little Richard and others. He quickly developed a reputation for his showy stage manner. In 1966, increasingly influenced by rock, he moved to London and formed a rock band with two white British musicians. Their band was called the Jimi Hendrix Experience and they played ferocious, shockingly loud rock with a strong foundation of electric blues. The charismatic Hendrix, a sensation in Europe, became an instant legend in the United States after his appearance at an outdoor festival in Monterey, California, in 1967.

Hendrix died just three years later, in 1970, from an accidental drug overdose. The records he made during his brief career, including *Are You*

*Jimi Hendrix is widely regarded as the greatest guitarist of all time. His unique and incredibly skillful playing has never truly been matched.*

*Experienced?* and *Axis: Bold as Love,* have inspired countless guitarists since. His fiery style, always testing the boundaries of what a guitar could do, created a legacy that many feel can never be matched. Rock critic John Morthland argued, "None has actually extended the directions he pursued, but perhaps that is because he took them, in his painfully short time on earth, as far as they could go."[45]

## Sly and Marvin: Boldly Political

Hendrix's music was revolutionary in a musical sense, but it was not often openly political. Many other black performers were more outspoken on the issues of the day, however. One such influential performer was Sly Stone, a keyboardist, singer, and songwriter from the San Francisco Bay Area.

Stone's earliest hits, including "Everyday People," were dance tunes with relatively mild social commentary. Stone's music became increasingly political, however, and his controversial 1971 album, *There's a Riot Goin' On,* used darker music and bold lyrics to address such subjects as racial violence, drug abuse, and armed uprising. By today's standards, the album does not seem revolutionary, but at the time, its radical nature caused an uproar.

Another musician to mix social commentary with music was Marvin Gaye, a longtime star in the Motown family of artists. His 1971 release, *What's Goin' On,* featured songs that openly and honestly addressed the issues of the day, such as the title track, as well as "Mercy Mercy Me (the Ecology)" and "Inner City Blues (Make Me Wanna Holler)." The album was much bolder, politically, than anything else Motown had ever done.

Motown's Berry Gordy generally disliked overtly political music, and at first refused to release *What's Goin'*

*On.* Gaye insisted on its release, arguing that he, as an artist, needed to push the boundaries of modern music. Though Gordy was hesitant to publish the record, *What's Goin' On* was a huge success with both the listening public and music critics everywhere. It became one of Motown's all-time biggest sellers.

## Stevie Wonder's Innovation

Marvin Gaye's success with *What's Goin' On* helped give another Motown star more artistic freedom. Stevie Wonder, equally gifted as a songwriter, singer, musician, and producer, became famous before he reached his teens. However, Motown strictly controlled every aspect of his professional life, from publishing and production to tour schedules and income. It has been estimated that by 1971, the singer had earned more than $30 million for Motown; he reportedly received only $1 million of that.

When Wonder turned 21 in 1971, he was able to negotiate a new contract with Motown. The result was millions of dollars in back royalties, along

with complete artistic control. He declared that he was "not interested in 'baby, baby' songs any more,"[46] and used his new freedom to create some of the most innovative and significant recordings in popular music.

Wonder's album releases during the 1970s, his golden years, included *Music of My Mind, Talking Book, Innervisions,* and *Songs in the Key of Life.* Some of his songs, such as "Don't You Worry 'Bout a Thing" and "You Are the Sunshine of My Life," extended Wonder's ongoing line of brilliantly

*Stevie Wonder innovated the music industry from a young age. He has a number of records that are considered classics and continue to get radio playtime well into the 21st century.*

melodic songs about love and family. Others, such as "Living for the City," reflected the singer's growing concern with social, political, and spiritual issues. Wonder's deep, widespread influence on pop music—touching virtually every aspect of singing, writing, playing, and production—would continue for decades.

## "Let's Stay Together"

As Wonder made hits in the North, in Memphis, Stax producer Isaac Hayes created such groundbreaking albums as *Hot Buttered Soul* in 1969 and the soundtrack album for *Shaft*, a controversial African American inner-city adventure film produced in 1971. This soundtrack won an Academy Award for having the Best Original Song.

The Memphis musical style was best represented during the 1970s by singer Al Green. Like many other black musicians of the era, Green got his start by performing in church. He later remembered the gospel he heard during his childhood in Arkansas: "It was put into my cornbread ... My mother and my father, they were Baptists. We were raised in church, and we sang at home ... I was just raised on the sound of Sam Cooke and the Soul Stirrers."[47]

Green also loved blues and R&B, but hid this enthusiasm from his family. When his secret was discovered, he struck out on his own and found success when he met Willie Mitchell in 1968, a producer and bandleader with whom he was stylistically in tune. Green combined his own compositions with Mitchell's quality production, which merged a solid core band with minimal horns and strings. Riding above it all was Green's unmistakable voice—a brilliant instrument that, similar to Ray Charles's singing, could take many different shapes. Green could ring out in falsetto, a breathless romantic croon, or a powerful shout with the passion of a gospel singer.

The result made him the decade's top soul musician, responsible for such classics as "Tired of Being Alone," "I'm Still in Love with You," and "Let's Stay Together." Then, at the height of his popularity, Green experienced a spiritual reawakening. In the mid-1970s, he became a minister, parted ways with Mitchell, and turned his back on the commercial music industry. He kept recording, however, developing a smooth, intimate sound for the gospel music he sang over the next several decades.

## The Philly Sound

Another distinctive 1970s style emerged from Philadelphia. It was a brand of infectious dance music called

Philly soul. Philadelphia International Records, the label behind Philly soul, was hugely successful, second only to Motown as an African American–owned record company. Among its biggest artists were the O'Jays, Harold Melvin and the Bluenotes, and Billy Paul. The label's chief architects were songwriters and producers Leon Huff, Kenny Gamble, and Thom Bell. They created a sound that was smooth, commercial, and heavily orchestrated, but also sensitive to the musical trends of the 1970s.

Lyrically, Philadelphia International Records leaned toward the inspirational. While the music was largely dance-oriented, the lyrics of typical Philly Sound songs were uplifting. Mark Anthony Neal noted:

> While producers of black popular music in past eras correctly understood the role of the black church as the dominant [force in the African American community], Gamble and Huff understood the role of the dance floor in the maintenance of black communal relations. Harking back to the 1930s and 1940s, [they] created dance-floor anthems [that] affirmed black communal and familial relations.[48]

## Disco Nights

Philly soul appealed strongly to dance fans, which formed a crucial link between the dance-and-romance soul of the 1960s and a style that had a brief, but powerful, few years of popularity in the mid-1970s. This was disco, a genre that is one of the symbols of the decade.

Disco's roots can be traced to the African American dance clubs of the 1950s, where people danced to records instead of live bands. In the 1960s, a European fad for these clubs, called discotheques, briefly swept through the United States. Celebrities, such as former first lady Jacqueline Kennedy, could be seen performing the latest dance steps in fashionable discotheques. In the early 1970s, similar dance clubs reappeared in cities all across the United States. These new clubs were initially associated with minority groups, mostly African Americans and Latinos.

Instead of a live band, a DJ provided music at a disco club. Their job was to play the hottest records, providing a soundtrack for nonstop dancing. Disco's basis was a relentless, pounding rhythm that stressed every beat. Anything could then be laid on top, from soulful vocals and Mozart melodies to wiggling synthesizer figures and screaming guitars.

For some time, disco remained

*Disco clubs quickly spread across America and produced an entirely new genre of music—even if it only stuck around for a few years.*

"one of the most popular and [hated] mileposts in pop music's history."[49]

## Dropping the Funk

As disco declined in popularity in the late 1970s, another musical style emerged. This new genre was called funk, a less polished genre that developed, at least in part, as a backlash to the extremely flashy style of disco. Funk also had clear roots in earlier genres. For example, it prominently used James Brown's method of combining multiple rhythms, staccato light horns, and heavy bass lines emphasizing the first beat of every measure. Funk also used elements of hard rock, such as screaming, Hendrix-like guitars, and wild keyboards borrowed from Sly Stone. It also incorporated newer elements, such as the recently invented synthesizer. This combination of past and present was deliberate, and many historians have pointed out that funk musicians were in tune with their musical roots. This was directly opposed to disco, which tried to be something brand new.

underground, but eventually it expanded far beyond its original audience and made stars of a number of singers and groups, black and white alike. Among these were Donna Summer, Gloria Gaynor, Barry White, Kool and the Gang, Abba, the Village People, and many others. Far and away the most successful were the Bee Gees, who supplied some of the music for *Saturday Night Fever*, a wildly popular disco film starring a young John Travolta.

The disco lifestyle, with its emphasis on drug use, glamour, and bold, unique fashion choices, faded after a few years, and so did the music. In its day, however, disco was a potent force. If nothing else, it provoked strong reactions of love or hate among music fans; author Mikal Gilmore noted that disco was

The prominence of a melodic bass in funk was symbolized by the fact that

# ACROSS RACIAL BOUNDARIES

Funk music, to a higher degree than most other styles, was inclusive of multiracial bands. One of funk's direct ancestors, Sly Stone, fronted a multiracial band. One of the top funk bands of the 1970s, Tower of Power, featured both black and white vocalists and instrumental horn soloists. Though there was undoubtedly still racial discrimination throughout the music industry, the racial divide between black and white musicians was beginning to close. Funk was one of the first mainstream genres to be openly and proudly multiracial. White and African American musicians shared the glory of their success equally and together. It was a sign that the racial unease in America was finally beginning to steady itself.

two of its foremost bandleaders were also bassists. Larry Graham played with Sly Stone for years before forming Graham Central Station; Bootsy Collins played with James Brown before creating Bootsy's Rubber Band. Among the many other prominent funk bands of the era were the Ohio Players, Tower of Power, and Earth, Wind, and Fire.

## "The Mothership"

All of these bands were distinctive, but for many fans, funk found its best expression in a wild and visionary man named George Clinton. Clinton was the genius leader of two overlapping groups, Parliament and Funkadelic. This extended family of musicians was referred to as P-Funk, and it had a number of hits starting in the mid-1970s, including "Give Up the Funk (Tear the Roof off the Sucker)" in 1976, "One Nation Under a Groove" in 1978, and "Atomic Dog" in 1982.

Clinton was a former Motown songwriter. Disapproving of the company's assembly-line approach to music, he was drawn to performers such as James Brown and Jimi Hendrix, unique individuals who went outside established boundaries to forge their own unique, individual sounds.

Clinton succeeded in creating his own style. A single P-Funk song might include Hendrix-style guitar freakouts, complex polyrhythms, jazzy horns, old-fashioned harmony vocals with roots in the gospel and spiritual traditions, and space-age electronics. P-Funk's live shows, meanwhile,

*A true individual, George Clinton was one of the revolutionary artists behind the development of funk music. His bold personality made him a major star.*

featured outrageous costumes and complex, flashy stage effects—such as a giant, saucer-shaped "mothership" from which the musicians emerged. Music writer Joe McEwen noted that this "mixture of tribal funk, elaborate stage props and the relentless assault on personal [limits] resembled nothing so much as a Space Age Mardi Gras."[50]

Holding it all together was Clinton's philosophy, which mixed racial pride with cosmic science fiction, romantic freedom, mythology, and more. Overall, P-Funk was great fun, but it also contained a serious message. Mark Anthony Neal noted, "Underlying much of the surface imagery of Parliament/ Funkadelic were sharp critiques of mass-culture, particularly within the realm of black popular music, and black nationalist [ideas]."[51]

## A Quiet Mixture

Of course, not all 1970s African American pop music was disco or funk. For example, one movement focused on extending traditional romantic aspects of R&B. Introspective love songs, with an emphasis on a smooth and highly commercial sound, reflected the style called quiet storm, named after a 1975 Smokey Robinson album. The quiet storm genre became popular enough that many radio stations adopted it as a specific format—a mixture of soulful ballads, easygoing jazz, and blues. Robinson, Teddy Pendergrass, Patti LaBelle, Peabo Bryson, Anita Baker, and Roberta Flack were among the most prominent performers of this mellow style. As the 1970s ended, another major shift began. Black pop music continued its evolution into the 1980s.

# CHAPTER SEVEN
## MAINSTREAM
## DOMINATION

**P**opular music in the 1980s was driven by individualism, both by the artists themselves and also by large multinational record labels. A few artists shattered barriers, both musically and culturally, with their unique styles, breaking into the mainstream and setting standards for influence and popularity that were unprecedented and would prove difficult for future acts to match.

### Top of the Pops
The biggest mainstream figure of the 1980s—indeed a pop culture phenomenon—was Michael Jackson. Jackson's family group, the Jackson 5, had been the last major act produced by Motown during the company's golden years. The pre-adolescent Michael's unbelievable singing and dancing made the Jackson 5 one of the label's most enduringly popular groups.

Not until Jackson went solo,

*After taking the world by storm in the 1980s, Michael Jackson put on energetic shows to sold-out arenas for decades.*

# MJ AND MTV

In the early 1980s, Michael Jackson was the first African American artist to benefit significantly from an exciting new phenomenon in popular music: the music video. Previously, MTV, the cable channel that introduced music videos to the world, had focused on reaching young white rock fans. Because of this, it had virtually ignored black artists. Of the 750 videos shown in the network's first year and a half, fewer than 24 featured black musicians.

Jackson destroyed racial barriers on the channel with videos like those accompanying his songs "Billie Jean" and "Thriller." They succeeded because they were not only visually compelling, but these songs were also incredibly popular. Jackson was a talented dancer, and his visual appeal was just as strong as his music. In addition, his production values were far beyond anything previously seen on MTV. Jackson's videos, which were elaborate and professionally produced, set high standards for future work in the medium.

however, did his career really explode. He and producer Quincy Jones struck gold with *Off the Wall* and *Thriller*. *Thriller* included collaborations with such different musicians as Toto and Eddie Van Halen, picked up eight Grammy Awards, remained one of the best sellers for more than a year, and became the best selling album in history. Its unprecedented success made Jackson a household name and earned him a new title: the King of Pop.

Among solo acts, Jackson's success was only approached by Elvis Presley, but unlike Elvis, Jackson toured the world extensively. Propelled by music videos and televised live performances, starting with *Thriller*, Jackson had tours for each of his albums. He visited dozens of cities around the world, with tens of thousands of breathless fans at each show.

## Prince

One musician who truly believed in artistry was Prince. He fused such elements as Hendrix-style guitar, punk rock, soul, and funk to create his own unique sound. Starting as a teenager in the late 1970s, Prince self-produced multiple demos and had record companies begging to sign him to long-term deals. He was able to secure record deals that included recording, production, and publishing rights, unheard of at the time for a teenage performer.

Prince combined an extreme talent for instrumentation with a desire to push boundaries, both musically and culturally. He could play every instrument he put his hands on. From guitars, drums, and bass to keyboards and piano, he was a gifted instrumentalist. Prince was also talented as a singer, with a powerful voice that had a wide range. He also wrote and produced music for women artists, such as Chaka Khan, Sheena Easton, and Sinead O'Connor. For many of his own songs, he increased the pitch of his singing to sing as his feminine alter ego,

*In the 1990s, a number of experimental groups were motivated by political and cultural issues. One of these bands was Rage Against the Machine, shown here in concert, which had both African American and white members.*

Camille. Always in tune with trending musical themes, Prince later incorporated hip-hop, new jack swing, and neo-soul into his songs.

His crowning achievement was *Purple Rain.* The film is a coming-of-age rock opera about a lead singer and featured sweeping ballads, hard rock, and electro pop. *Purple Rain* and its soundtrack album won two Grammy Awards and the Academy Award for Best Original Song Score. Though Prince passed away in April 2016, his legacy of musical innovation will live on in the music of countless artists inspired by him. In the days after his death, dozens of musicians across the world paid tribute to his life.

Spurred by Prince's success in rock music, other African American artists started finding opportunities in the genre. Living Colour found success in the late 1980s and early 1990s with hard rock songs inspired by the politics of the day. Bad Brains' fast-grinding punk and Fishbone's spirited combo of rock and other genres attracted devoted fans. The music and politics of these bands influenced Rage Against the Machine, a multiracial rap-rock band that found wide acclaim for using experimental instrumentation in combination with political statements, creating rap-rock as its own genre.

# A TRUE MUSICIAN

Prince was a musical genius. Not only did he write the vast majority of his songs, but he also played nearly all his own instruments on his first five albums. He used multi-tracking technology to play and record each instrument independently. He then layered them on top of each other. His drum programmer, Fafu, claimed he never once saw Prince make a mistake. At concerts, Prince would switch from guitars to other instruments throughout his performance.

Even other professional and accomplished artists were impressed with Prince's incredible musical talent. When asked by radio personality Howard Stern if Prince was a better musician than him, Foo Fighters front man and former Nirvana drummer Dave Grohl said Prince was a better overall musician, drummer, and singer than he was.

## Beats, Rhymes, and Life

One of the most significant developments in African American pop music during the 1980s and 1990s was the explosive rise and mass acceptance of hip-hop and rap. This music radically de-emphasized melody and harmony, stripping away virtually everything except rhythmic beats and spoken, or rapped, vocals. The term "hip-hop" originally referred to the entire lifestyle the music represented, while rap referred to the music itself. Today the genres are used interchangeably.

Besides the extreme reduction of melody, hip-hop also had unusual instrumentation. Originally, rap music did not use conventional instruments, relying instead on record turntables and drum machines to create rhythms. In time, rap also incorporated more sophisticated technology, such as sampling—repeating small bits of other songs for rhythmic effect—and live instrumentation.

As with earlier musical movements, such as bebop, hip-hop developed far from the mainstream, originating as a rebellion against traditional styles. Also like bebop, hip-hop was part of an entire urban lifestyle that embraced specific, ever-changing fashions, dance styles, slang, and art.

## Creating a Base for Hip-Hop

Hip-hop began in the New York City

# SUPER SHOWCASE

The Super Bowl is an American cultural hallmark. Every year, it is the most watched program on U.S. television and viewed by millions all across the globe. From the 1990s on, the NFL has hired rock and pop stars to play the Super Bowl halftime show, which is the highest-profile performance imaginable. Michael Jackson (1993), Diana Ross (1996), and Prince (2007) all had solo performances in halftime shows. Featured in others were James Brown, Stevie Wonder, Queen Latifah, Boyz II Men, The Temptations, Smokey Robinson, and Beyoncé.

Outshining them all was R&B singer Whitney Houston, and she did not even perform in the halftime show. In 1991, Houston sang "The Star-Spangled Banner" before Super Bowl 25 in Tampa, Florida. With the First Gulf War underway, it was the first Super Bowl broadcast during wartime in almost 20 years. Her moving rendition stirred the nation and became one of the highest-selling versions of the national anthem ever. Released twice, soon after the Super Bowl and then after the September 11, 2001 terrorist attacks, Houston's version of "The Star-Spangled Banner" generated proceeds that were donated to charity.

*Whitney Houston's performance of "The Star-Spangled Banner" at the 1991 Super Bowl, shown here, was a perfect example of her powerful voice.*

borough of the Bronx in the late 1970s. Using massive sound systems, a group of young DJs from Jamaica played dance records at parties. One of these was DJ Kool Herc, today acknowledged as the music's primary original innovator.

Herc's big break came when he noticed that dancers enjoyed certain moments in records more than others. Everyone wanted these breaks—brief segments when everything but the

# RAP'S DEEP ROOTS

Music historians and scholars have taken an interest in the hip-hop movement ever since it took hold in the late 20th century. The unique and difficult lives of inner-city African Americans were exposed in the new genre, and many of its original artists took inspiration from their African heritage:

*The idea of rapping has deep roots in African American culture. Its stylistic and thematic predecessors are numerous: the dozens and toasting traditions from America and Jamaica; sing-song children's games; double-dutch chants; black vernacular preaching styles; the jazz vocalese of King Pleasure, Eddie Jefferson, and Oscar Brown Jr.; the on-the-air verbal virtuosity of black DJs; scat singing; courtship rituals; the lovers' raps of Isaac Hayes, Barry White, and Millie Jackson; the politicized storytelling of Gil Scott-Heron and the Last Poets; and the preacherly vocables of Ray Charles, James Brown, and George Clinton, among many others.*[1]

1. Guthrie P. Ramsey Jr., *Race Music: Black Cultures from Bebop to Hip-Hop.* Berkeley, CA: University of California Press, 2003, p. 165.

percussion dropped out—to last as long as possible. Herc found he could sustain a break indefinitely by using two turntables and two copies of the same record, cutting quickly back and forth between the two.

Words spoken over microphones, often by two or more people, were added to the beats. This was similar to toasting, a tradition from Jamaica in which DJs talked in rapid-fire, semi-improvised rhyme, over music. Similar practices appear elsewhere in black musical history, and the tradition can be traced back to ancient African poetry.

## Defining a New Genre

Younger musicians, such as Afrika Bambaataa, Grand Wizard Theodore, and the Cold Crush Brothers, modified Herc's ideas. Some added sung vocals over the beat. Others experimented with scratching—manually moving a record back and forth on a turntable to produce rhythms—or used an electronic drum machine.

Gradually, these rappers, sometimes called MCs, took equal space in the spotlight along with DJs. MCs spoke directly to the audience. Over the DJs' rhythms, they improvised spoken lyrics in which they commonly boasted about their skills, wealth, and lifestyles, or mocked other rappers.

The style took shape within a context of social strife. The poorer neighborhoods of New York in the 1970s could be frightening and dangerous, with high rates of crime, gangs, and drugs. For young African Americans and Latinos drawn to the hip-hop scene, the music—which frequently had positive, uplifting themes—was their response to this environment. The hip-hop lifestyle offered impoverished African Americans a way out of a dangerous life.

## "The Message"

Rap stayed relatively underground for some time. Its creators remained local and their only recordings were homemade cassette tapes that circulated around the Bronx and nearby neighborhoods. Although later rap would become associated with money and violence, the music in these early days was mostly about fashion and good-natured competition between groups. Everyone was competing to have the best lyrics, the most popular mixes, or the biggest crowds for their performances.

In 1979, the first rap recordings came out: "King Tim III," by the Fatback Band, and a surprise hit, "Rapper's Delight," by the Sugarhill Gang. In 1982 came "The Message" by Grandmaster Flash and the Furious Five. Mark Anthony Neal noted that this song earned critical attention for its blunt comments, perceived by the listening public as genuine, about the struggles of inner-city life. Millions of listeners, of all races, had never truly been exposed to the struggles of poor African Americans; rap music changed that.

Hip-hop began to spread, with small groups of performers and fans emerging across the country. Its popularity took a huge jump in the mid-1980s with *Raising Hell*, an album by Run-DMC that had notably aggressive lyrics and music. A highlight was "Walk This Way," Run-DMC's collaboration with members of the white rock band Aerosmith. The song's clever music video showed the groups on opposite sides of a wall, playing different versions and making each other angry—and then tearing down the wall and jamming together.

## Mainstream Recognition

"Walk This Way" appealed to white

*Will Smith (left), now one of the biggest entertainers in the world, first appeared as one half of the hip-hop duo DJ Jazzy Jeff and the Fresh Prince, shown here.*

rockers and black hip-hoppers alike; it helped bring rap to a wider, mainstream audience, and the genre's popularity exploded in the following years. Rapper Kurtis Blow appeared in a soft drink commercial, MTV started a popular show called *Yo! MTV Raps*, and performers such as LL Cool J and Slick Rick scored major hits. The music's presence in the mainstream was cemented when the first Grammy Award for rap was given in 1988 to a pop-oriented duo, DJ Jazzy Jeff and the Fresh Prince

(Will Smith).

Many rap pioneers fought against this newfound massive popularity. Some believed that making money and acquiring fame was "selling out," or abandoning the values that had been the basis of hip-hop. They complained that the music no longer belonged to a select few and that it was being weakened to appeal to a wider audience. Russell Simmons, cofounder of the record label Def Jam, said of the move to the mainstream: "Hip-hop didn't cross over from black to white. It crossed over from cool to uncool."[52]

On the other hand, the move to the mainstream can be seen as a natural progression of events for any musical style. Historian Nelson George said: "Twenty-first century hip-hop is an industry with institutions, [standards], and [codes]. That's cool. That's evolution. That's life."[53]

## Coast Versus Coast

As its popularity increased, rap split into subgenres. One was relatively tame and commercial, represented by such acts as DJ Jazzy Jeff and the Fresh Prince and MC Hammer. Otherwise, rap was roughly divided into two camps, centered on the West and East Coasts.

Broadly, East Coast rap placed a greater stress on social, spiritual, and political awareness, urging its listeners to study history and current issues. Public Enemy's thought-provoking *It Takes a Nation of Millions to Hold Us Back* was an example of this approach. Other East Coast rappers included the Fugees, who combined catchy pop with politics, and the Wu-Tang Clan, who mixed hardcore street-style rapping with references to kung fu. Not every East Coast rapper believed in using the music to further political awareness, however. For instance, Sean "Diddy" Combs pioneered the use of a successful rap career as a springboard to running a massive retail and business empire.

West Coast rap, meanwhile, generally reflected aspects of "gangsta" life—the inner-city black lifestyle, with its ongoing problems of poverty, neglect, drug abuse, violence, and crime. Among West Coast rap artists were Ice-T and N.W.A., whose album *Straight Outta Compton* was the first mainstream gangsta rap album. Following N.W.A.'s breakup in 1992, several members pursued solo careers. Among them was Dr. Dre, whose album *The Chronic* was released in 1992 to great critical and commercial success. Dr. Dre went on to become a top producer of rap records and even created his own line of high-end headphones. Similarly to Diddy, he used his career as a rapper to create a

*One of the hip-hop community's most influential and respected members was Tupac Shakur. When he was murdered in 1996, many observers began to worry about the violent content in some rap music.*

business worth billions.

Fueled by the media attention on rappers, a rivalry between East and West Coast rappers developed during the 1990s. Rivalries had long existed in the world of hip-hop, but were generally no more serious than good-natured competitions between musical competitors. However, 1990s rap feuds turned violent. This resulted in, among other tragedies, the still unsolved murders of two top performers: Tupac Shakur and the Notorious B.I.G.

# AN EXPANDING GENRE

Over the years, the scope of rap has widened considerably. For example, although its artists were once almost exclusively male, many important female rappers have emerged over the years. They range from the first woman to make a solo rap record—Lady B. in 1980—to such artists as Nicki Minaj, Salt-N-Pepa, Lil' Kim, Missy Elliott, and Queen Latifah. A number of significant white rappers have also found success, including the Beastie Boys, Macklemore, Mac Miller, and the extremely successful Eminem.

## Controversial Sounds

The increasingly violent lyrics of many rap songs caused controversy across the United States. Tipper Gore, wife of politician Al Gore, accused rap of promoting the glorification of materialism, racism, and misogyny (hate toward women). This sparked the creation of advisory stickers for albums that contained explicit language.

Rap is not the first African American music genre to be controversial, it is simply the latest. Journalist Christopher John Farley pointed out, "All major modern musical forms with roots in the black community—jazz, rock, even gospel—faced criticism early on."[54] Defenders of rap note that rap is a flexible means of communication, adaptable for many situations and messages. As such, it connects communities that might otherwise be isolated, instantly bringing them news, ideas, and information. Chuck D, founder of the rap group Public Enemy, has famously referred to rap as "black America's CNN."[55]

## R&B's New Swing

In the late 1980s, African American pop music had increasingly mixed classic soul and R&B with hip-hop. Indeed, there has been little recorded black popular music in recent years that has not been influenced at least somewhat by hip-hop. One example was the movement called new jack swing. This subgenre incorporated elements from a diverse range of traditionally black musical styles, such as jazz, funk, rap, and R&B.

Often, entirely new melodies and arrangements were created. Sometimes, the music borrowed from existing songs, sampling bits from classic R&B or soul tunes and playing

*Janet Jackson launched a highly successful career as a singer and entertainer. Her album* Rhythm Nation 1814 *showcased her ability to combine multiple genres.*

them over hip-hop beats. Among key producers and performers in this style were Babyface, Boyz II Men, Destiny's Child, R. Kelly, Toni Braxton, TLC, Mary J. Blige, and Usher.

Janet Jackson incorporated new jack swing on her groundbreaking album *Rhythm Nation 1814*. Prior to this album, Jackson had largely been regarded as a pop singer stuck in the shadow of her older brother Michael. Produced by Jimmy Jam and Terry Lewis, who had previously worked with Prince, *Rhythm Nation 1814* dealt with social issues such as homelessness and poverty, with songs in genres ranging from new jack swing to hard rock, quiet storm, and more. Her long-form video, or "telemusical," featuring three songs from the album, pushed the music video format to new heights. *Rhythm Nation 1814* is the only album to chart No. 1 hits on the Billboard Top 100 in three separate years.

Hip-hop has also influenced current trends in gospel music. A new genre, broadly called contemporary gospel, combines the spiritual message of traditional sacred music with modern beats. Among its most gifted performers are Kirk Franklin, Donnie McClurkin, and Yolanda Adams.

These artists have tried to make gospel's sound current without compromising its ancient religious messages. Adams, recalling her early apprenticeship with Houston's Southeast Inspirational Choir, said: "We were trying to make sure young people enjoyed gospel music, so we had really fresh beats and songs kids could sing along with when they heard them the first time. We were teen-agers; you wouldn't expect us to sing ... like Mahalia Jackson sang in 1940."[56]

## Maintaining a Classic Sound

Meanwhile, the many other styles that have developed from the foundations of black popular music have continued to flourish. Among the prominent examples are Irma Thomas, the smoky-voiced Queen of New Orleans R&B; traditionally minded acoustic bluesman Keb' Mo'; soul legend Solomon Burke; and Robert Cray, a guitarist, songwriter, and singer influenced by R&B and blues.

Jazz has enjoyed periodic surges in popularity over the decades, though it has never achieved the massive audience it had during the swing years. Over the decades, it has combined with funk, merged with rock, and passed through a period of free jazz, in which traditional concepts such as meter, chord changes, and melody were stripped away or modified.

Trumpeter Wynton Marsalis is dedicated to keeping the sounds of jazz alive for future generations. Marsalis, part of a prominent New Orleans musical family, was the first person of any race to win Grammy Awards in both jazz and classical music on the same night. In his role as a champion of classic jazz, Marsalis has been key in establishing a musical ensemble, based at New York City's Lincoln Center, dedicated to keeping the music of composers such as Duke Ellington alive. Marsalis's efforts have inspired similar groups all around the country.

# CHAPTER EIGHT
# MUSIC FOR TODAY AND TOMORROW

Hip-hop has created a dizzying number of stylistic subgenres and variations. Some of these have strong regional flavors. For example, OutKast, of Atlanta, Georgia, became hugely popular with a distinctively southern style incorporating a rhythm called southern bounce. Miami bass, trap, and crunk are three more subgenres that emerged from the South.

Like pop music in the 1980s, rap in the 2000s and onward became more personality-driven. A handful of artists with remarkable talent and huge personalities have not only set the course for African American music, but also gained strong representation and power, controlling recording labels, album sales, and music distribution across the globe.

## Neo-Soul

An R&B movement that arose in the 1990s to early 2000s was neo-soul, a reimagining of 1970s soul music that was influenced by 1990s hip-hop. Inspired by 1990s predecessors A Tribe Called Quest and De La Soul, artists such as D'Angelo, Erykah Badu, Jill Scott, Macy Gray, and Lauryn Hill sang about modern black life, incorporating spiritual and political consciousness with emotion and soulful wit. Neo-soul artists have worked with hip-hop acts such as the Roots, Mos Def, Talib Kweli, Common, and others.

## Two Titans of Hip-Hop

Two of the biggest hip-hop artists of the 21st century, Jay Z and Kanye West, have had intertwining careers and contrasting backgrounds. Jay Z grew up in the impoverished Marcy Projects in Brooklyn, while Kanye West grew up in Chicago with a mother who was a professor. Embracing their differences, the two have fueled hip-hop for more than a decade. After starting Roc-A-Fella

# A TRUE ORIGINAL

A fixture in hip-hop and neo-soul is the Roots, a band started in Philadelphia in the late 1980s by rapper Black Thought and drummer Questlove when they were in high school. The Roots combine rap with live instrumentation, which

sets them apart from their contemporaries. Their 1999 album *Things Fall Apart* (named after the novel by Chinua Achebe) combined jazzy grooves, rapping, and heightened social consciousness that highlighted issues in the music industry. The Roots also produced music for Erykah Badu, D'Angelo, and others, and backed up Jay Z for performances on *MTV Unplugged* and at Lincoln Center. Eventually, they reached such acclaim that Jimmy Fallon selected the Roots to be the house band for *The Tonight Show*.

*As the drummer and cofounder of the Roots, Questlove has built a unique public image for himself. He is widely regarded as a groundbreaking musician.*

Records, Jay Z had huge hits such as "Can I Get A ..." and "IZZO." He eventually worked with West, who produced songs for Jay Z's album *The Blueprint*.

Getting his start producing songs for other artists, West was initially regarded as a beat maker and had trouble starting his rap career. He combined hard and cinematic beats with high-pitched soul sample hooks inspired by producers RZA (from the Wu-Tang Clan) and J Dilla. He got his big break after making the song "Through the Wire," which was about breaking his jaw and having it wired shut after a car accident. This led to two groundbreaking albums, *The College Dropout* and *Late Registration*, which topped charts worldwide and won multiple Grammy Awards.

Jay Z continued to influence music not only as an artist, but also as an

# THE NEPTUNES' PLANET

When it comes to production outfits, it is hard to top the Neptunes duo: Pharrell Williams and Chad Hugo. The production team made more than 20 number-one hits from the late 1990s to the early 2010s. *Billboard* named them the top producers of the 2000s. Their vast production catalog features collaborations with Justin Timberlake, Britney Spears, Gwen Stefani, Busta Rhymes, Missy Elliott, and the Neptunes' own band, N.E.R.D.

Williams has gone on to have a highly successful solo career as a singer, collaborating with such artists as Daft Punk, Snoop Dogg, and 2 Chainz, and having hit songs, such as "Happy," featured in film soundtracks. He also served for four seasons as a judge and coach on *The Voice*.

entrepreneur. Through his own label, Roc-A-Fella Records, and also during his three-year presidency of Def Jam Recordings (2004 to 2007), Jay Z helped enhance the careers of singers, such as Rihanna and Grimes, and rappers, such as West, Big Sean, and Rick Ross. He also helped change how music is listened to when he founded Tidal, a platform for streaming music, which was introduced in late 2014. Like Jay Z, West started his own record label, GOOD Music, working with artists such as John Legend, Kid Cudi, Pusha T, and Desiigner. Jay Z and West would release a duo album called *Watch the Throne* in 2011.

## Emotional Rap

Already at the top of the pop music world, West impacted the entire genre of hip-hop with his 2008 release *808s and Heartbreak*. He created minimalist beats using a Roland TR-808 drum machine and samples. He overlaid confessional, Auto-Tuned vocals, mixing singing and rapping, throughout the album. Other rappers had sung hooks before, such as Ja Rule, Buckshot from Black Moon, and Nelly, while Andre 3000, Mos Def, and Lauryn Hill often alternated between singing and rapping on songs on their albums. However, none of these artists had combined the two vocal styles with so much success.

With such a huge departure from his earlier work, and with much more singing than rapping, *808s and Heartbreak* initially received mixed reviews. In retrospect, the album broke new ground with its emotional expression and experimental production. As a result, *808s and Heartbreak* birthed the emo-rap subgenre, popularized by singer-rappers, such as Drake, Kendrick Lamar, and Chance the Rapper; Auto-Tuned singers, such as T-Pain and Future; and trap-singers, such as Fetty Wap and Travis Scott.

## Beyond Beyoncé

At the same time as West and Jay Z, other rappers made a major impact on popular music in the 2000s and 2010s. Lil Wayne's dark, gritty, and humorous takes on rap and celebrity living gave spirit to his *Tha Carter* trilogy of albums. Young Jeezy and Rick Ross revitalized the trap subgenre. Rap remains an integral part of American popular culture, the current dominant style of African American music, and a powerful influence on music worldwide.

After her start in the girl group Destiny's Child, Beyoncé racked up 13 Top 10 Billboard Hot 100 hits. This success included five number-one hits: "Crazy in Love, "Single Ladies," "Irreplaceable," "Baby Boy," and "Check on It." Her soulful voice and signature dance routines in videos and onstage have captivated millions. Her

popularity spread to the silver screen as she acted in movies such as *Dreamgirls* and *The Fighting Temptations*.

In 2016, Beyoncé released the masterpiece *Lemonade*. The album and accompanying "visual album" were released with little advance notice. The album was released with music videos for each song, and her storytelling in these videos is similar to the style Michael Jackson and Janet Jackson used in the 1980s and 1990s. The music of *Lemonade*, which features both trap beats and soaring choruses, deals with her personal relationship struggles and triumphs (Beyoncé is married to Jay Z), southern black identity, as well as police brutality, especially on

*In genres dominated by popular male rappers, Beyoncé has made a name for herself by taking a number of innovative approaches in her music. Her albums have been influenced by jazz, blues, rap, neo-soul, and many other genres.*

the song "Formation," which she performed at the Super Bowl 50 halftime show. *Lemonade* debuted on Billboard as the top album, making Beyoncé the only artist to have six albums debut at number one.

## The Future of African American Music

Black artists continue to find audiences for work beyond rap and R&B genres. TV on the Radio's sultry vocals and fresh sound are embraced by indie/electro rock fans, many of whom also enjoy the edgy soul rock of singer Santigold. Gnarls Barkley had a massive hit with "Crazy," which combined soul singing from CeeLo Green with beats from Danger Mouse. Janelle Monáe, nicknamed the Electric Lady, is making her own path through modern R&B, funk, '60s revival, neo-soul, hip-hop, electro pop, and everything in between.

African American popular music has amassed a deep and colorful legacy that spans more than a century. This legacy is celebrated in "Musical Crossroads," a permanent exhibition at the Smithsonian National Museum of African American History and Culture in Washington, D.C.

Of course, black music is not just a museum piece, frozen in time. It is ever-changing, evolving as African American musical genius continues to innovate and the music-loving public catches on.

# NOTES

## Introduction: A Century and a Half of Music

1. Quoted in Eileen Southern, *The Music of Black Americans: A History.* New York, NY: Norton, 1997, p. 575.
2. Merriam-Webster Online, s.v. "blue note," accessed February 28, 2017. www.merriam-webster.com/dictionary/blue%20note.

## Chapter One: Black Music's Beginnings

3. Robert Darden, *People Get Ready!: A New History of Black Gospel Music.* New York, NY: Continuum, 2004, p. 1.
4. Southern, *The Music of Black Americans*, p. 5.
5. Quoted in Southern, *The Music of Black Americans*, p. 48.
6. Quoted in Southern, *The Music of Black Americans*, p. 84.
7. Quoted in M. Shawn Copeland, "Wading Through Many Sorrows," in *Womanist Theological Ethics: A Reader*, ed. Katie Geneva Cannon, Emilie Maureen. Louisville, KY: Westminster John Knox Press, 2011, p. 148.
8. "Follow the Drinking Gourd"— African American Spiritual. Houghton Mifflin Harcourt Social Studies Primary Sources. www.eduplace.com/kids/socsci/nyc/books/bke/sources/bkc_template.jsp?name=spiritual&bk=bkc&state=ny.
9. Southern, *The Music of Black Americans*, p. 92.
10. Julius Lester, *Black Folktales.* New York, NY: Grove Weidenfield, 1969, p. 113.
11. Horace Clarence Boyer, *The Golden Age of Gospel.* Chicago, IL: University of Illinois Press, 2000, p. 19.

## Chapter Two: Bringing a New Era

12. David A. Jasen and Gene Jones, *That American Rag: The Story of Ragtime from Coast to Coast.* New York, NY: Schirmer, 2000, p. xxiv.
13. Quoted in Mark Anthony Neal, *What the Music Said: Black Popular Music and Black Popular Culture.* New York, NY: Routledge, 1999, p. 8.
14. Southern, *The Music of Black Americans*, p. 317.
15. Quoted in Joslyn Pine, *Book of African-American Quotations.* Mineola, NY: Dover, 2011, p. 105
16. Quoted in Giles Oakley, *The Devil's Music: A History of the Blues.* Cambridge, MA: Da Capo Press, 1997, p. 104.
17. Quoted in Southern, *The Music of Black Americans*, p. 332.
18. Quoted in Jack Chambers,

*Milestones: The Music and Times of Miles Davis.* Toronto, ON: Da Capo Press, p. 209.

19. Jasen and Jones, *That American Rag,* p. xxxvii.

20. Quoted in Rudi Blesh, *They All Played Ragtime: The True Story of American Music.* New York, NY: Alfred A. Knopf, 1950, p. 90

## Chapter Three: Swinging and Bopping

21. Quoted in John Edward Hasse, *Beyond Category: The Life and Genius of Duke Ellington.* New York, NY: Simon & Schuster, 1993, p. 404.

22. Whitney Balliett, "Celebrating the Duke," *New Yorker*: November 29, 1993, p. 136.

23. Southern, *The Music of Black Americans,* p. 391.

24. Quoted in Nat Shapiro and Nat Hentoff, ed., *Hear Me Talkin' to Ya: The Story of Jazz as Told by the Men Who Made It.* Mineola, NY: Dover, 1955, p. 350.

25. Dizzy Gillespie and Al Frazer, *To Be, or Not—to Bop.* Garden City, NY: Doubleday, 1979, p. 201.

26. Quoted in Fox, *Showtime at the Apollo,* p. 137.

## Chapter Four: Rhythm and Blues, Rock and Roll

27. Quoted in Reiland Rabaka, *The Hip-Hop Movement: From R&B and the Civil Rights Movement to Rap and the Hip Hop Generation.* Plymouth, UK: Lexington Books, 2013, p. 103.

28. Quoted in Hirshey, *Nowhere to Run: The Story of Soul Music.* London, UK: Southbank, 2006, p. 23.

29. Ramsey, *Race Music,* p. 64.

30. Quoted in *Rolling Stone* editors, *The Rolling Stone Interviews,* 1967–80. New York, NY: Rolling Stone, 1981, p. 224.

31. Quoted in Grace Lichtensteinand Laura Danker, *Musical Gumbo: The Music of New Orleans.* New York, NY: W.W. Norton & Company, 1993, p. 98.

## Chapter Five: Music for the Soul

32. Quoted in Hirshey, *Nowhere to Run,* p. 315.

33. Quoted in DeCurtis and Heinke, *The Rolling Stone History of Rock & Roll,* pp. 260–261.

34. Quoted in Darden, *People Get Ready!* p. 245.

35. Whitney Balliett, *American Singers: 27 Portraits in Song.* New York, NY: Oxford University Press, 1988, p. 57.

36. Quoted in Jon Pareles and Bernard Weinraub, "Ray Charles, Bluesy Essence of Soul, Is Dead at 73," *New York Times,* June 11, 2004, p. A1.

37. Quoted in Adam Woog, "At his 75th birthday, Sam Cooke still sends us," *Seattle Times,* 2006. old. seattletimes.com/html/entertainment/2002749834_cooke20.html.

38. Quoted in Tony Fletcher, *In the Midnight Hour: The Life and Soul of Wilson Pickett*. New York, NY: Oxford University Press, 2017, p. 28.

39. Quoted in Craig Werner, *Higher Ground: Stevie Wonder, Aretha Franklin, Curtis Mayfield, and the Rise and Fall of American Soul*. New York, NY: Crown/Archetype, 2007.

40. Peter Guralnick, *Sweet Soul Music: Rhythm and Blues and the Southern Dream of Freedom*. New York, NY: Little, Brown, 1999, p. 332.

41. Quoted in Patricia Romanowski and Holly George-Warren, eds. , *The New Rolling Stone Encyclopedia of Rock & Roll*. New York, NY: Rolling Stone, 1995, p. 839.

42. Quoted in Rolling Stone, *The Rolling Stone Interviews*, 1967–80, p. 71.

43. Arthur Kempton, *Boogaloo: The Quintessence of American Popular Music*. New York, NY: Pantheon Books, 2003, p. 216.

44. Quoted in Jon Landau, "Otis Redding, King of Them All" in, William McKeen, ed., *Rock and Roll is Here to Stay: An Anthology*. New York, NY: W.W. Norton Company, 2000, p. 492.

## Chapter Six: Moving and Grooving into the Seventies

45. Quoted in DeCurtis and Heinke, *The Rolling Stone History of Rock & Roll*, p. 418.

46. Quoted in Ramsey, *Race Music*, p. 2.

47. Quoted in Fred Bronson, *The Billboard Book of Number One Hits: The Inside Story Behind Every Number One Single on Billboard's Hot 100 from 1955 to the Present*. New York, NY: Billboard Books, 2003, p. 306.

48. Neal, *What the Music Said*, pp. 119–120.

49. Mikal Gilmore, *Night Beat: A Shadow History of Rock & Roll*. New York, NY: Doubleday, 1998, p. 242.

50. Quoted in DeCurtis and Heinke, *The Rolling Stone History of Rock & Roll*, p. 523.

51. Neal, *What the Music Said*, p. 103.

## Chapter Seven: Mainstream Domination

52. Quoted in Kempton, *Boogaloo*, p. 441.

53. Quoted in Jim Fricke and Charlie Ahern, *Yes, Yes, Y'all: The Experience Music Project Oral History of Hip-Hop's First Decade*. Cambridge, MA: Da Capo Press, p. ii.

54. Quoted in Jared Green, ed., *Rap and Hip-Hop*. San Diego, CA: Greenhaven, 2003, p. 90.

55. Quoted in Alex Eichler, "Rap Isn't 'Black America's CNN,'" *The Atlantic*, October 12, 2010. www.theatlantic.com/entertainment/archive/2010/10/rap-isn-t-black-america-s-cnn/339862.

56. Quoted in Darden, *People Get Ready!* p. 313.

# FOR MORE INFORMATION

## Books

Frankl, Ron. *Miles Davis: Musician and Composer*. New York, NY: Chelsea House, 2014.
This book is a detailed and thoroughly researched look at one of the most celebrated African American musicians of all time, Miles Davis.

Fricke, Jim and Charlie Ahern. *Yes, Yes, Y'all: The Experience Music Project Oral History of Hip-Hop's First Decade*. New York, NY: Da Capo, 2002.
An interesting oral history of early hip-hop, told through the words of its pioneers and heavily featuring photos, this book also has reproductions of flyers and other primary sources.

Grady, Cynthia and Michele Wood. *Like a Bird: The Art of the American Slave Song*. Minneapolis, MN: Lerner Pub Group, 2016.
This work takes a look at some of the deepest origins of African American music—slave songs—and provides a foundation for understanding the later movements of jazz, soul, and hip-hop.

Orr, Tamra. *Drake*. Kennett Square, PA: Purple Toad Publishing, 2014.
This in-depth look at one of rap's biggest stars in the 2010s showcases his early life and how he built success through new media platforms.

Pinkney, Andrea Davis. *Rhythm Ride: A Road Trip Through the Motown Sound*. New York, NY: Roaring Brook press, 2015.
This interesting book examines the history of the Motown record label, including details about some of its biggest stars and hits.

## Websites

**Archives of African American Music and Culture (aaamc.indiana.edu)**
Curated and maintained by Indiana University, this site has links to pictures, videos, and short articles that explain the rich history of African Americans in music.

**"The Challenge of Presenting "African American Music": First, Define It" (www.washingtonpost.com/entertainment/music/the-challenge-of-presenting-african-american-music-first-define-it/2016/09/20/e6ec6f8c-711d-11e6-8533-6b0b0ded0253_story.html?utm_term=.9fa68188f518)**

This well-researched article describes the difficulties faced by musical historians as they try to uncover the roots and foundations of African American musical traditions.

**Honor! A Celebration of the African American Cultural Legacy (www.carnegiehall.org/honor/history)**

Created by professionals at Carnegie Hall, a famous musical auditorium, this site has in-depth information about a wide variety of genres influenced by African Americans.

**Museum of Pop Culture (www.mopop.org)**

This is the official site of the Museum of Pop Culture, located in Seattle, Washington; it has information about its exhibits, many of which showcase the influential and innovative African American traditions in music.

**National Museum of African American Music (nmaam.org)**

This website has links to multimedia sources that explore the history of African Americans in different genres of music, including specific information about the museum's exhibits.

# INDEX

# PICTURE CREDITS

# ABOUT THE AUTHOR

**Andrew Pina** writes and edits on a freelance basis. He has written books about sports and government, and has written and edited for websites covering football and college sports. Andrew has also edited educational, nonfiction, and reference books and materials covering music, crafts, history, science, math, and a wide array of other subject matter. Andrew has lived in the United States, France, South Korea, and Canada. In South Korea, he taught at Moonhwa High School, a college preparatory boarding school in the historic and beautiful city of Gyeongju. Andrew enjoys traveling, languages, and learning about different cultures. Today, he resides in Toronto, Ontario, Canada.